What others are saying about . . .
The Inside Out Youth Worker™

"I believe in the authors of *The Inside Out Youth Worker*. Their approach to ministry is fresh, biblical, and hope-filled. Birthing and growing an effective student ministry is indeed an art and always begins inside the heart of a leader. This book creatively takes youth workers to the inner core of ministry and moves them on a journey from being a disciple to making disciples. Read it, apply it, live it—and students will become world shaking authentic followers of Christ!"

—**Dan Webster,** Founder, Authentic Leadership, Inc.

"I love this approach to thinking about ministry! There are aspects of great youth ministry that can best be described as Art; but the Work is inescapable, and no less important. By pairing these concepts and fleshing them out under practical umbrellas, Kent and his capable team of writers have created an excellent addition to any youth worker's reading and thinking diet."

—**Mark Oestreicher,** President, Youth Specialties

"*The Inside Out Youth Worker* has its heart in exactly the right place—namely, that the best youth ministry 'strategy' is the power of a transformed life. Kent Julian and friends expose a notorious ignorance in youth ministry—that it's possible to deeply impact teenagers using 'tips and techniques' that are disconnected from our own transformation. This book is both practical and challenging, and will not only upend the way you see ministry, but might just change your life."

—**Rick Lawrence,** Executive Editor, GROUP Magazine

"When you think about youth ministry, you probably think first about what you can see—the activity, the noise, the silliness, the coolness, the sheer outrageousness. But Kent Julian and his outstanding writing team remind us that effective youth ministry has less to do with what is on the outside than what is on the inside. The heart and soul of youth ministry is to be found in the heart and soul of the youth leader. This excellent book is about excellent youth ministry leadership—without which there can be no youth ministry at all. This is a must-read for every adult who feels called to work with kids."

—**Wayne Rice,** Professor of Youth Ministry, San Diego Christian College, Co-founder of Youth Specialties, and banjo player extraordinaire

"Radiating a spirit of collaboration, this practical and insightful book will undoubtedly help youth workers, the veteran and new recruit alike, more fully realize what it means to develop followers of Jesus—from the inside out."

—**Chris Folmsbee,** President, Sonlife Ministries

"The bottom line in youth ministry is not how many kids you have coming to your group but rather, where they will be 10 to 15 years from now. This book and its message will help you prepare students to be lifelong followers of Christ. Kent Julian and his very experienced youth ministry specialists have done an outstanding job helping us understand the 'being' art and 'doing' work of making disciples.

—**Jim Burns, PhD,** President, HomeWord

"In a time when too many youth workers are searching for the right 'formula' to imitate, *The Inside Out Youth Worker* celebrates an individual's originality. It's a great reminder that God is first concerned with who we are which then flows into what we do. Youth workers spend too much time developing their gifts while neglecting their character. Programs and giftedness may impress people, but true character changes people. I love the way this book keeps the priority on character, yet gives us plenty of practical tips on running a ministry."

—**Francis Chan,** Lead Pastor, Cornerstone Church in Simi Valley, California, and President, Eternity Bible College

"*The Inside Out Youth Worker* is as fresh as last week's youth worker lunch conversation and as significant as Youth for Christ's current strategic planning priorities. The authors have tackled the right topic at the right time, and my prayer is that the Lord will bury this important message in our hearts—the only location that will make a difference.

—**Dr. Dave Rahn,** V.P. of Ministry, Youth for Christ/USA

"A deep yet practical book, *The Inside Out Youth Worker* is great for the full-time youth pastor as well as the noble volunteer. Kent, along with a host of contributors, addresses many core issues that are overlooked in other youth ministry resources. And regarding issues that are addressed in other sources, we are given fresh and unique insight. I highly recommend *The Inside Out Youth Worker* and plan to urge my youth ministry students to read it as well!

—**Leonard Kageler, PhD,** Chair of the Youth Ministry Department, Nyack College

"With so many youth ministry books focusing on 'doing' instead of 'being,' programming instead of people, and the power of humanity instead of the power of God, *The Inside Out Youth Worker* takes us into a completely new direction that is much needed today. Get ready to be encouraged and challenged to rethink what it means to 'make disciples' and how it all begins from the inside out. Youth workers will be blessed by this book—I know I was!"

—**David Chow,** Author of *The Perfect Program and Other Fairy Talks*, and Founder, Leading Together

"Over the years the pendulum has admittedly swung too far to the programming side of youth work which solicited an abundance of literature out today that overcompensates. Kent Julian's *The Inside Out Youth Worker* does not do so. Making the most of several well respected practitioners of the 'art' of youth work, Kent presents a well balanced, biblical approach to youth ministry that not only catches the mechanical aspects of working with teenagers, but also the intangible nuances. This book balances both the character and the competence needed for youth ministry, and I believe it will radically refocus the face of ministry for generations."

—**Jeff Piehl,** Student Ministries Team Facilitator, Evangelical Free Church of America

"As a student ministries pastor, I've found countless books that are about building a ministry worth attending, but this book stands out by helping youth workers become leaders worth following. *The Inside Out Youth Worker* is a compelling look at how the inner life of a youth leader shapes the feel, flavor, and health of a youth ministry. Filled with sharp insights and innovative application, this book will be a valuable read for anyone who is into leading the next generation toward Christ."

—**Kevin Queen,** High School Pastor, Crossroads Community Church in Lawrenceville, Georgia

"*The Inside Out Youth Worker* is a biblically based and practical resource with cutting-edge relevance. This book contains a wonderful balance of warmth and depth—the best book of its kind I've read in years!

—**Dan Reiland,** Executive Pastor, Crossroads Community Church in Lawrenceville, Georgia, and former V.P. of Leadership and Church Development, INJOY

"The typical youth worker is overwhelmed with ministry tasks—phone calls, e-mails, planning, meetings—the 'to-do' list is seemingly endless. Oftentimes, the result is that we end up neglecting our most significant role: inviting and guiding young people into discipleship with Jesus. That is why this book is so important. This wise team of youth ministry veterans calls us back to our true passion and the reason why we got involved in youth ministry in the first place. They remind us that the discipleship of young people begins with our very own discipleship to Jesus."

—**Brett Kunkle,** Student Impact Speaker for Stand to Reason

The Inside Out Youth Worker™

Discovering the ArtWork of Making Disciples

Kent Julian
General Editor

Life-On-Life Publishers

The Inside Out Youth Worker: Discovering the ArtWork of Making Disciple

Copyright © 2006 by Kent Julian

Published by Life-On-Life Publishers
Lawrenceville, GA

CREDITS:
Cover design by Matt Archer of New Mosaic Media
Interior design by Charles Sutherland
Edited by Kent Julian and Amy Raubenolt

Subject Headings: Youth Ministry
  Youth Ministry Leadership
  Youth Ministry Training
  Youth Discipleship

All rights reserved. No part of this publication may be reproduced, stored in a retrieval system, or transmitted in any form or any means—for example, electronic, mechanical, photocopy, recording, or any other—without the prior written permission of the publisher. The only exception is brief quotations in printed reviews.

Printed in the United States of America

ISBN 0-9777363-0-X

Library of Congress Control Number: 2006901228

Includes bibliographical references

Unless otherwise indicated, Scripture quotations are from: the HOLY BIBLE, NEW LIVING TRANSLATION®, (NTL). Copyright © 1996 by Tyndale Charitable Trust.

Special discounts are available in quantity purchases by churches and Christian organizations. Requests for information should be addressed to Life-on-Life Publishers, 1210 Steeple Run, Lawrenceville, GA 30043 or by e-mailing *lifeonlife@earthlink.net*.

dedication

This book is dedicated to the incredible youth ministry volunteers that each of the contributing authors has had the privilege to serve alongside. Our lives are richer because of you! You've helped us smile, laugh, and discover the transformational power of inside out youth ministry. Thanks for pressing on—your commitment to serving Christ by loving teenagers inspires us.

contents

About the Authors — xi

Acknowledgements — xv

Forward by Rick Lawrence, Editor, GROUP Magazine — xvii

Introduction

Chapter 00: Before We Begin — 1

Chapter 01: Making Disciples—The ArtWork of Inside Out Youth Workers — 5

Part 1: The Art of BEING

Chapter 02: The Art of Character — 21

Chapter 03: The Art of Balance — 35

Chapter 04: The Art of Confidence — 49

Chapter 05: The Art of Intentionality — 67

Chapter 06: The Art of Priority — 86

Part 2: The Work of DOING

Chapter 07: The Work of Context — 105

Chapter 08: The Work of Affection — 121

Chapter 09: The Work of Contacting — 138

Chapter 10:	The Work of Resolution	154
Chapter 11:	The Work of Teaching	171
Chapter 12:	The Work of Programming	188

Conclusion

Chapter 13:	Inspiring True ArtWork—You Get What You Expect	211

Notes 214

about the authors

Matt Archer is a 15-year veteran of youth ministry and also serves as the creative director of New Mosaic Media, an organization committed to developing visual resources for youth ministry. A popular speaker and trainer, Matt desires to equip youth workers to connect with teens by engaging their culture. Matt is currently the Pastor of Student Ministries at Snoqualmie Valley Alliance Church in Washington. He and his wife Rachelle reside in Snoqualmie with their three daughters.

Mike Harder has been in youth ministry for 19 years. He enjoys running, reading, sports, mission trips, and speaking at retreats, conferences, and training events. He and his wife Teresa live in the Philadelphia metro area with their three children—Nathan, Lauren, and Arianna. Mike is presently the youth pastor at Branchcreek Community Church where he gives oversight to the Middle School, High School, and Young Adults Ministry, and is also a Sonlife Ministries trainer.

Kent Julian, the primary author and general editor of *The Inside Out Youth Worker*™, served in local church youth ministry for over 15 years and is currently the National Director for Alliance Youth Ministries. Kent is a sought after speaker around the country, trains for Sonlife Ministries and GROUP Magazine Live, and has contributed to several books and numerous magazines. However, to really know Kent, you need to know that some of his favorite pastimes include hanging out with his incredible wife, Kathy, and their three awesome children, exercising, eating sushi, and sipping skim milk lattes at Starbucks.

Chris Lankford served in youth ministry for over 18 years, most recently at Neighborhood Church in Castro Valley, California. He is currently the Lead Pastor at Long Beach Alliance Church in Long Beach, California, and is a Sonlife Ministries trainer. His passions include theology, teaching God's Word, Starbucks, golfing, and avoiding vegetables. He is married to the love of his life, Melinda, and has two wonderful daughters.

Melinda Lankford has worked with both junior high and high school students for 11 years and especially enjoys ministry to female youth volunteers. She has been married to Chris for 11 years, is the mother of Jessalyn and Makayla, and lives in Long Beach, California. She loves being transparent with her own shortcomings in order to show students the transformational work of Christ in her life. She is currently the Women's Ministry Coordinator at Long Beach Alliance Church, along with being the pastor's wife and raising their two girls.

Jason Ostrander is a youth pastor who most recently served in Moses Lake, Washington. He is married to his best friend, Calu', and they have a son named Liam. Jason grew up in Philadelphia, Pennsylvania, and moved out to the Pacific Northwest following his college graduation. Actually, Jason drove from the east coast to the west coast and ran out of money in Washington. Five moves, four jobs, three dogs, two homes, and one wife later, God called him into full-time youth ministry. Jason is currently pursuing a master's degree in Theology at Regent College in Vancouver, B.C.

Lee Towns is currently the Student Ministry Team Leader at Fellowship Bible Church in Little Rock, Arkansas. He and his wife Carla have been married 22 years and have two daughters, Ashlee and Carlee. Lee is a Sonlife Ministry trainer, a graduate of Toccoa Falls Bible College, and has been in student ministry for 20 years. He has served in churches in New York, Florida, California, and North Carolina.

Guy Wasko has been in the trenches of student ministry for over seven years and is currently the Pastor of Student Ministries at Westwood Church in Orlando, Florida. He is a big picture thinker that doesn't forget about the details. Aside from loving to lounge by his pool with his wife Rebecca and daughter Emma, he also enjoys the beach, reading, hanging out with students, and traveling. Guy received a Masters in Practical Theology and an MA in Organizational Leadership from Regent University in Virginia and also is a trainer for GROUP Magazine Live.

Erik w/a "k" Williams was born in Munich, Germany, with dual citizenship from Norway and the United States. Erik spent a good portion of his early years moving around with his military family, but spent his teenage years in upstate New York, where he landed at Houghton College for college studies. After serving as a youth pastor in Georgia and then as a middle school pastor in Salem, Oregon, he is now the Director of Next Generation Ministries for the Christian and Missionary Alliance in the Pacific Northwest. He loves to surf, snowboard, play guitar, speak, and be with his amazing wife Jeanne-Ann and children Kynzi and Karston.

John Zivojinovic (aka "Z-Man") is passionate about honoring God. The important ways this is revealed in his life is by being married to Teresa for 22 years, being a father to his three daughters (Tarah, Kaitlin, and Tori), and being a student ministries pastor for 20 years, most recently at Grace Chapel in Englewood, Colorado. He finds being a novice philosopher, theologian, and social scientist stimulating and his two biggest hobbies are collecting books and getting degrees. John is also a Sonlife Ministries trainer and a popular speaker at camps, retreats, and conferences.

acknowledgements

Thank you to all nine contributing authors—Matt Archer, Mike Harder, Chris Lankford, Melinda Lankford, Jason Ostrander, Lee Towns, Guy Wasko, Erik w/a "k" Williams, and John (Z-Man) Zivojinovic—not only are you all great writers, you are inside out youth workers to the core! Your vision and excitement for this book has equaled mine. I admire how each of you has a heart for God and a passion for students. Even more, your friendship and ministry partnership over the years has meant the world to me.

Thank you to Matt Archer for your creativity and talent in designing the cover.

Thank you to Charles Sutherland for your excellent interior design work.

Thank you to Amy Raubenolt, our editor. It has been a joy to work with you.

Thank you to the many youth ministry volunteers who the authors have worked alongside with over the years. Your influence has contributed significantly to this book.

Thank you to the families of each contributing author. Deadlines are a bear, and I'm sure you helped the writer in your home stay true to them.

Thank you to my wife, Kathy, and my kids, Christopher, McKenzie, and Kelsey, who cheered me on during many nights and weekends of editing and reediting and reediting. I love doing life with all four of you!

Most of all, thank you to our Lord and Savior Jesus Christ. All the authors are forever grateful for your grace and goodness.

Kent Julian
December, 2005

forward

Not long ago I was meeting with some of my GROUP Magazine team members to discuss youth ministry strategy—we were fishing around for common threads in each other's own stories of transformation. I asked my teammates to talk about the spots along their life's timeline when real transformation happened.

One said his life changed when he spent a day in a canoe with his church's worship pastor, fishing on a mountain lake. I asked him to focus on what was actually transformational about that day. He thought for a minute, and then said it must have been the slow, unhurried pace of the day. I responded, "You could have had a slow, unhurried day with almost anyone—was it the slowness of the day or the person sitting across from you in the canoe?

"Well, it was that worship pastor, of course," he said.

"What was it about him that set the stage for transformation in your life?"

There was an uncomfortable silence while he searched for the intangible "right answer." Finally, a little bewildered, he said, "I guess I don't know."

I think most of our transformational moments happen in the context of relationships with people who can "bring the wood"—I mean people who've been transformed *by* Jesus and are therefore *like* Jesus. It's their Christlikeness—Jesus Christ living unfettered through them—that surprises us, challenges us, and opens us to healing.

But, like my teammate, it's hard to put our finger on exactly why some people move through life leaving a wake of transformation behind them while others don't. And that brings us to *The Inside Out Youth Worker*™.

When I became editor of GROUP Magazine 18 years ago, there were far fewer youth ministry resources available, and even fewer good youth ministry resources. Now we're glutted by hundreds of books, CD-ROMs, DVDs, and online resources—most of them really great. We've become quite skilled at our "tips and techniques" in youth ministry. But somewhere along the line we've forgotten that real impact flows through a transformed life. And that's exactly what Kent Julian and his team of writers are going after in this book.

St. Francis of Assisi famously said: "Lord, make me an instrument of your peace; where there is hatred, let me sow love; where there is injury, pardon; where there is doubt, faith; where there is despair, hope; where there is darkness, light; and where there is sadness, joy."

What does it mean to be made into an "instrument" God can use to transform lives? How do we "sow" the fruit of the Spirit? Well this book will walk you down that road. It's an unusual book for youth workers because it dives into the intangibles that deeply impact others and makes them tangible. It's a book to be savored, not skimmed.

So find yourself an open day, a canoe, and a mountain lake—or some reasonable facsimile. Invite Jesus to sit across from you. Then read this book together. I think you'll come away from your day transformed.

                Rick Lawrence
                Executive Editor, GROUP Magazine

before we begin
by Kent Julian

Go and make disciples . . .

Jesus Christ

If you've worked with teenagers for more than, say…a month, you've probably heard some interesting comments. *What did you say you're doing? You're braver than me; I could never work with* **those** *kids. Are you a glutton for punishment or just stupid? I can think of better things to do with my time—like putting my head in a vise.*

When reading the title of this book, *The Inside Out Youth Worker*™, you might think I'm just another guy taking a shot at you. Nothing could be further from the truth. Calling you an inside out youth worker is the finest compliment I could give. Let me explain . . .

why this book?

This book, from start to finish, is about making disciples of Jesus Christ among teenagers. Yet, unlike many youth ministry books about disciple-making, this one doesn't focus on programs, processes, systems, or structures. It's about you—the youth worker. The authors included in this compilation passionately believe that the starting point for any discussion about making disciples in youth ministry is with youth workers themselves—who they are and what they should be about. Getting it right here is 80% of the battle. Miss this and the most strategic programs will matter very little. Being inside out is that important!

Therefore, this book zeroes in like a laser beam on our heroes—youth workers who are in-the-trenches. Whether you are full-time, part-time, or a volunteer, our intention is to inspire and challenge you to be inside out. Each idea we share has been critical to our long-term health and effectiveness in youth ministry, and after you finish reading, we hope you will be able to say the same.

a few helpful hints

Instead of viewing this book through how-to lenses, I encourage you to read it as if we were "talking shop" at our favorite coffee house. Imagine sitting down in an overstuffed chair with your favorite drink. The aroma in this place is robust and fresh. Soft jazz music is playing in the background. It simply feels good to be here. At first, we discuss the latest strategies and ministry tools. After a while though, we get down to what matters most—how are we *doing* at making disciples? Even more, how are we at *being* disciples? We get gut-level honest, and the stories we share become the fertile soil in which passion and commitment for Christ and his commission grow.

While reading, occasionally remind yourself that this book is about you, the youth worker, not youth ministry itself. While it's packed with ideas about creating the right environment in ministry, there aren't many thoughts on programming or structure. Currently, my plan is to write two more books within this series entitled *The Inside Out Youth Ministry*™ and *The Inside Out Teenager*™. These will wrestle with the important issue of programs, but that is not the focus of this book. This book deals with something more important—you!

In addition, even though this is a book about you and dedicating a few chapters to talking about the development of a personal vision statement would fit well within its parameters, we have deliberately chosen not to include such chapters. We made this choice because the intent of this book is to describe how inside out youth workers *purposefully live* rather than to address the more theoretical topic of how to develop a personal vision statement. Since there are a number of solid resources currently available concerning the development of personal purpose such as *The Path* by Laurie Beth Jones, *Visioneering* by Andy Stanley, and the classic *Seven Habits of Highly Effective People* by Stephen R. Covey, we recommend you read one of these books to flesh out your vision statement and use this book to determine how to practically live out your vision within the realm of youth ministry.

It's also important to realize that while we don't write as experts who have arrived, we do believe our insights are solid. When assembling this team of authors, I looked for youth workers in different life stages with different experiences. However, the one area in which difference was not tolerated was in the authors' passion and commitment to making disciples through an inside out approach. No wiggle room was allowed here. What this means is that while we don't have all the answers, we do have many. Each of us is dedicated to being inside out. We aren't arrogant or cocky about it, we just believe that God, in his grace, has taught us some important lessons through our commitment to inside out principles. We feel compelled to share these thoughts, not because we have it all together, but because putting pen to paper helps us process what God has done and is doing in our lives. As a result, we believe the ideas in this book will help you in your inside out journey. As the nineteenth century theologian Tyron Edwards once wrote, "If you would thoroughly know anything, teach it to others."[1]

Finally, don't rush through this book. Although it is an easy read, it is not a shallow read. Take your time. Stop and reflect. Meet with others and discuss the questions at the end of each chapter. Yet even though we encourage you to go slow, don't go too slow. Do something with what you read. Take action! There is no perfect time or situation to start anything, so just start. Too often we busy ourselves reading books and attending seminars, but before we have a chance to implement what we've learned, we're reading the next book or attending the next seminar. Stop the cycle! Do something with the information in hand. Pick one principle to reinforce every day for three months. "Research now shows that if you repeat a behavior for 13 weeks . . . it will be yours for life."[2]

our hope

Our hope is that this book changes your life. Notice, I didn't say our hope is that this book will change your youth ministry. We hope it will change *you*! We fervently believe that if you look at life through inside out lenses, you will change. Not only that, but as you change, we believe you'll automatically experience change in youth ministry as well. That's what happens when you dedicate yourself to being inside out.

So together, let's start the journey to becoming inside out youth workers!

01

making disciples

the ArtWork of inside out youth workers

by Kent Julian

I want to touch people with my art.

Vincent Van Gogh

I'm no artist.

My eight-year-old daughter, Kelsey, is naturally artistic, but she didn't pick it up from dear old dad. For me, stick figures are a challenge. Kelsey, on the other hand, instinctively knows how to use shapes and colors. Even at a young age, she has the ability to see something and transfer that image from her eyes to her hand. I can see the same thing, but nothing noteworthy moves from my eyes to my hand. Most things . . . no, everything . . . gets lost in transition.

So here's a question: Why does a non-artist like me choose the term "artwork," intentionally misspell it by capitalizing the "w," and then use it as a descriptive term in this book? What does a non-artist know about ArtWork?

making disciples

As stated in the introduction, this book is about one thing—making disciples of Jesus Christ among today's teenagers. For me, as well as the other authors, seeing students follow Christ is a consuming passion. Nothing thrills us more than when Jesus calls a teenager to himself and that teen pursues Christ with abandonment. It leaves each of us speechless!

Yet, even more, Christ has extended an invitation to each of us and to you to join him in calling teenagers to himself. This means that although it is Jesus who changes lives, we can get in on the action. How? By responding to his disciple-making commission . . .

> *Jesus came and told his disciples, "I have been given complete authority in heaven and on earth. Therefore, go and make disciples of all the nations, baptizing them in the name of the Father and the Son and the Holy Spirit. Teach these new disciples to obey all the commands I have given you. And be sure of this: I am with you always, even to the end of the age." (Matthew 28:18-20)*

why the special focus?

You might wonder why we place so much emphasis on the phrase "make disciples." There are a bunch of other action words in Matthew 28:18-20, so why the special focus? Aren't "go," "baptizing," and "teach . . . to obey" just as important? The answer, surprisingly, is both yes and no.

When Jesus told his followers to make disciples, he wasn't making a suggestion. He wasn't saying, "Hey Peter, James, and John, may I recommend disciple-making? It's worth considering. Andrew and Philip . . . want to get in on this action?" It wasn't like that at all. When Jesus instructed his followers to make disciples, he was issuing a command. In fact, out of all the action words in these verses, this is the only imperative. "Make disciples" is a direct decree. Authoritative. Mandatory. Binding. Obligatory. Jesus was saying, "If you are going to follow me, then making disciples is not optional."

But what about the other action words? Aren't they marching orders as well?

Not exactly.

The other action words are participles. If you're rusty on your grammar, I'll remind you; participles are verbal adjectives that give active descriptions to a word or phrase. In this case, the participles "go," "baptizing," and "teach to obey" describe key actions associated with making disciples. These participles are important words, but they're not the most important words. The main character of this play is "make disciples"; "go," "baptize," and "teach to obey" are the supporting cast. They are the words that explain how.

graduation day!

Another important insight about this passage is the context. If you've graduated from high school or college, think back to your graduation. For most of us, it was a pretty special day. We dressed up in robes and square hats. Speeches were given. People were recognized. Parties were thrown. Why all the hoopla? Because graduation was a big deal! It was a day to recognize the completion of our diploma or degree. Massive amounts of time, energy, and money were invested in earning that diploma so, of course, a celebration was in order. Yet graduation wasn't just a day of completion, it was also a day to acknowledge our preparedness. We were not just *moving away* from something, we were *moving toward* something—something more, something fuller. There was a new season of life ahead, and we were ready.

Do you remember, by chance, your commencement speaker? Can you recall his or her name? How about the message? More than likely, your commencement speaker said something like this: "Over the past few years, you have experienced _____, faced _____ challenges, gained knowledge in _____, and built _____ kinds of relationships. All these things have prepared you for what lies ahead. Now, go and do _____!"

Have you ever considered that Jesus' last words to his followers were his commencement speech? Think about it . . . many of his disciples had been with him for close to three years. They had experienced miracles, healings, parades, parties, storms, confrontations, persecution, and the death and resurrection of their leader. They had walked dusty roads with Jesus, laughed with him, cried with him, and shared their dreams with him. Through all their experiences, both the highs and the lows, they had built a personal relationship with the God of the universe. Then, just before ascending into heaven, in a commencement address to his faithful followers, Jesus basically says, "Because of all of these experiences and challenges, because of the Kingdom insights I've shared with you, and because of the relationships we have built, it's time for you to graduate into something more, something fuller. It's time for you to make disciples!"

what is a disciple?

So what exactly was Jesus asking his followers to do? What is a disciple and how are they made? It might surprise you that the biblical concept of discipleship is not nearly as intricate as modern Christianity has made it out to be. In its most basic definition, a disciple is a pupil or learner. Yet in Jesus' day, disciples were not educated in the same way we are educated today. Instead of sitting in a classroom, disciples attached themselves to a master teacher called a rabbi. It was sort of like an apprenticeship, but again, very unlike most apprenticeships offered through colleges or highlighted on TV. The relationship between a rabbi and his disciple was radical. "The disciple left his home and moved in with his teacher. He served the teacher in the most servile ways, treating him as an absolute authority. The disciple was expected not only to learn all that his rabbi knew, but also to become like him in character and piety (Matthew 10:24; Luke 6:40). The rabbi in return provided food and lodging and saw his own distinctive interpretations transmitted through his disciples to future generations."[3]

With this in mind, when Rabbi Jesus commissioned his followers to make disciples, he was throwing down a huge challenge. He was saying, "Cultivate believers who are as attached and committed to me as you are." How committed were his original believers? Very! All of them had weaknesses and moments of stumbling, but they were all devoted to Christ and his cause. Most were put to death for their beliefs, and following him took precedent over everything else in their lives. They loved Jesus more than self, spouse, children, parents, or friends. It was more than a high-level commitment, it was the ultimate commitment.

the ArtWork of making disciples

Up to this point, what I've covered has probably been a review for most readers. Nothing new or earth-shattering. Nevertheless, perhaps you're wondering, "What does ArtWork have to do with making disciples? And, while you're at it, why the funky spelling?"

Good questions! First, allow me to share a few random thoughts, and then I'll move on to answering these questions. The answers won't be earth-shattering, but perhaps they'll stimulate deeper conversation.

random thoughts

As already indicated, while the biblical concept for making disciples is simple, Christians have complicated and formalized it over the centuries. For instance, when I say "youth discipleship," the vision that comes to mind for many Christians is a group of teenagers meeting once a week, sitting on a linoleum floor in the fellowship hall, and filling in blanks in blue notebooks. Yet this scene is disconnected from the scenes Scripture describes. Granted, some transfer of knowledge might happen during these meetings—if that's possible while sitting on linoleum—but how does such a picture relate to "attaching" oneself to Rabbi Jesus? Once-a-week meetings aren't even in the same ballpark as "doing life" with Jesus.

Additionally, Jesus commissioned his followers to "go and make disciples." This means even the term "discipleship," as we understand it today, is warped. Discipleship nowadays usually gets defined as growing closer in one's relationship with Christ. It's easy to fit the participles "baptize" and "teach to obey" into this picture, but shouldn't the picture also include the other participle? Isn't there room for "go?"

Obviously, "go" should fit into one's definition of discipleship, but if we're honest, in most churches, it doesn't. Instead, discipleship focuses on things like how Christ can help us overcome temptation, be joyful, and become more successful. These applications aren't necessarily bad, just basic. If the end result of discipleship stops with what Christ can do for us, it is ultimately immature and selfish. Jesus taught that the closer we get to him, the less focused we'll be on ourselves and the more our eyes will do what his eyes do—turn outwardly towards others. This means discipleship should eventually lead to serving others and evangelism. However, in most cases, the journey down the discipleship path usually ends up leading to another, "deeper" Bible study on a different linoleum floor.

new specs

It is these random thoughts that led me to gather a number of authors who, like me, see discipleship through different lenses. We see Christ's commission as more . . .

- fluid than formulaic;
- organic than organized;
- self-investing than self-ingesting, and
- a relational connection than a rigid content.

It's not that there's no room for formula, organization, or personal growth, we just believe these elements should occur within the framework of doing life with Christ. For the most part, it's the *context* of making disciples, not necessarily the *content*, that we view differently.

Hence, when deciding to write a book about our passion for making disciples among teenagers, we wanted to use a word or phrase that painted a fluid, organic, self-investing, relational picture. Through discussion with the other authors, as well as a moment in time watching my daughter draw, it dawned on me that the word we had to use was "Art-Work."

the ART of being

Art is usually defined as a product of human creativity—such as the creation of a beautiful painting or sculpture. Additionally, it is sometimes defined as a superior skill, like the art of negotiation, which can be learned through study and practice. However, there is another definition rarely used today that describes the first of the two core elements essential for anyone who wants to respond to Christ's disciple-making commission. Here's the definition, "The second person singular, indicative mode, present tense, of the substantive verb *be*. (i.e. thou 'art') . . . Now used only in solemn or poetical style."[4]

Kind of technical, isn't it? But did you get the gist of it? "Art," in solemn and poetical writing, can mean "are," as in "you are kind" or "you are gracious." In these instances, "art" speaks of traits or characteristics that are central to a person's *being*. For example, check out how "art" is used in the following phrases from the King James Version of the Bible:

- "for thou art stiff-necked people" (Deuteronomy 9:6)
- "For thou art a holy people unto the Lord, thy God" (Deuteronomy 14:2)
- "And Achish answered and said to David, I know that thou art good in my sight, as an angel of God" (1 Samuel 29:9)
- "Wherefore thou art great, O LORD God: for there is none like thee, neither is there any God beside thee" (2 Samuel 7:22)

In these verses, "art" does not speak of paintings, sculptures, or developed talents; it addresses inner qualities that are core to someone's being. That is what we are referring to when we talk about the *art of being*—central, internal attributes deep within an individual's soul. Moreover, the art of being speaks of things God builds into a person. Although we should strive to do our part in developing our being, we must realize it is God who inwardly shapes and transforms us. The things we do—the spiritual disciplines, the reading, the time given to reflection—are crucial to spiritual formation, but let's be clear, the art of being has much more to do with what God does within us than any practice we initiate. Our efforts create space for God, yet it is God who does the internal work.

the WORK of doing

The second core element for responding to Christ's disciple-making commission—the work part—is a bit easier to grasp. We get this. We've heard tons of sermons and read numerous books about what it takes to make disciples.

But do we really get it? If you're like me, you've understood *what* you are supposed to do, but you've wrestled with *how* to do it? For years, I struggled with trying to find the best way to make disciples in youth ministry. Despite all the seminars, books, and sermons, the *how* question remained. I tried the three easy steps, seven habits, and every irrefutable law ever written. Seriously, you name it, I've tried it, but nothing really delivered. Fewer and fewer disciples were being made.

Have you had a similar experience?

Ever wonder why?

Just as with the art of being, I discovered that how I make disciples is not so much about what I do, as it is about what God accomplishes. Make sure this sinks in. Chew on it. Think it through. Even the work of making disciples is primarily God's responsibility. Let me explain . . .

The doing side of making disciples takes a lot of effort. For instance, consider all the work Paul did to advance Christ's movement. There were sleepless nights. Thousands of miles were traveled. Presentations were made. Persecution was endured. Dozens, if not hundreds, of letters were written. On the whole, his work week was easily 60 hours plus. Yet, all his work was environmental.

Whoa!

Slow down.

Don't miss what was just written.

Read it again . . . carefully.

All his work was environmental.

Making disciples is not—I repeat, not—about us transforming people into followers of Christ. That's the Holy Spirit's job. Our role is to create an environment in and around our lives that opens up opportunities for God to call people to himself. That's it! Nothing more. It's about what he does *through* us, period! His Spirit performs the heart surgery; we simply prep the operating room. The sooner we fully embrace this, the sooner we are freed from the unnecessary burden of feeling like it is our responsibility to change the hearts of teenagers.

Don't get me wrong, I'm not promoting a passive, wimpy, "let go and let God" style of Christianity. What I am saying is that when it comes to making disciples, in a real sense, we don't make them. No matter how hard we try or how powerful our programs are, we cannot cause a single student to follow Christ. But, as stated earlier, we can join God in what he is doing in the lives of students. We can do our part to create an atmosphere in our lives and ministries that allows teens to soak in the truth of God.

art + work = ArtWork

As you can see, ArtWork, and even its funky spelling, has everything to do with making disciples! It speaks of the two core elements essential for any youth worker wanting to respond to Christ's commission. If you break it down:

> **The ART of Being** is about character formation. It involves the first half of the Great Commandments—"love the Lord your God with all your heart, all your soul, and all your mind" (Matthew 22:37)—and refers to what God does on the *inside* of youth workers. Even though we should strive to love God with our entire beings and develop the right inward characteristics, it is important to understand that it is God who actually does the transforming. Our efforts are purely a means of creating space for God to work within us.
>
> **The WORK of Doing** involves the second half of the Great Commandments—"love your neighbor as yourself" (Matthew 22:39)—and refers to what youth workers do on the *outside* to make disciples. Loving others is an overflowing by-product of loving God with our entire being, but again, it's essential that we understand our role in loving teenagers. Our role is not the transformation of students; that's God's role. The role we play is the creation of environments in and around our lives that open up opportunities for God to call teenagers to himself. It's all about Christ working through us.

These two elements, the art of being and the work of doing, are both environmental. The first creates the right atmosphere in us; the second creates the right environment around us. Together, they create the ArtWork of making disciples.

the inside out youth worker

When I watch Kelsey draw, I'm amazed. As I've said, I'm no artist. Even if I wanted to be, there is nothing artistic inside me. It's simply not there. I remember art class as a kid; no matter how hard I tried, my pictures always ended up looking like something other than their intended object. Fruit looked like a multicolored glob. Trees looked like green globs. Animals . . . brown globs. Buildings, you guessed it, gray globs. If it wasn't a stick figure, it came out glob-ish. But with Kelsey, it's different. There's something artistic inside her that bubbles to the surface when she draws. It's in there, at her core, and when given the opportunity, it rises. She will have to work to hone her skills, but the fundamental elements already exist.

The same can be said about inside out youth workers. There is something inside them that bubbles to the surface when they're around students. It's in there, at their core, and when opportunities present themselves, it emerges. They have to work to hone their skills, but the fundamental elements already exist.

what's an inside out youth worker?

What is it that bubbles to the surface of inside out youth workers? For one, inside out youth workers are passionately committed to the art of being. They are disciples themselves—learning followers attached to Rabbi Jesus. Like Jesus' early disciples, they have weaknesses and moments of stumbling, but without a doubt, they are devoted. They love Christ more than self, spouse, children, parents, or friends. Additionally, they realize that it is Christ who shapes and transforms their insides. Although they are highly committed to practicing spiritual disciplines, they see their efforts as simply a way to create space for God.

Inside out youth workers are also committed to the work of doing. As disciples who make disciples, they have embraced Christ's invitation to join him in calling teenagers to himself, and they see this work as a primary outward calling of their lives. However, even though they are passionate about this calling, they have thrown in the towel when it comes to trying to change teenagers. Instead, they focus on the environments in and around their lives and leave the transforming to God.

Ultimately, what makes youth workers inside out is that they have discovered the proper order of ArtWork. For most Christians, the work of doing takes precedence over the art of being. But for inside out youth workers, being comes first. They understand they are human beings, not human doings, and, at their core, they believe God accomplishes more *through* them when they are open to what he wants to do *in* them.

> *Instead of trying to please others, I have learned to live my life for an audience of One. Doing God's work isn't as important as being God's person. . . . Strengthen your youth ministry by placing a higher priority on being than doing.*
>
> Doug Fields
> high school pastor at Saddleback Church
> from his book
> *Purpose Driven Youth Ministry*

let's be clear . . .

Today, many youth workers talk about making disciples. Some even say they are committed to being before doing. However, an honest look at the state of youth ministry in America reveals a picture that isn't too positive. The picture isn't bleak; it's just not nearly as colorful as it could be. We have more paid professionals, more training, more resources, more websites, and more books than we need . . . and fewer disciples than we should.

Why?

The authors of this book believe one of the main reasons the results in youth ministry today are less than stellar is that most youth workers struggle with living inside out. They want to live a being-before-doing lifestyle, but they simply don't know how. This is why we felt so compelled to write. We've been there! For years, most of us misunderstood our role and tried, in our own power, to transform ourselves and others. But each of us has experienced a breakthrough and is beginning to live inside out. We don't have all the answers, but this inside out approach is enabling us to ask better questions. We're moving in the right direction and believe the concepts written in these pages can help you be both a better disciple and a better disciple maker.

where we go from here

The rest of this book is divided into two sections. The first section focuses on the first priority—the art of being. It addresses inner qualities like character, balance, confidence, intention, and priority. By no means is this list comprehensive, we've simply picked qualities we believe are of great significance for youth workers. In addition, the traits we concentrate on are ones that we believe are more fluid than rigid. When fleshed out together, they should help you process life better, in spite of all its craziness and messiness.

While reading this section, please remember to view everything through environmental lenses. It is God who transforms us, not any particular action. As we've said, actions simply create space for God to work within us. Therefore, remember to put on your "environmental specs" before reading.

Additionally, we have stayed away from writing chapters on prayer, personal devotions, fasting, solitude, simplicity, and other classic spiritual disciplines. Although these disciplines are central to the art of being, we've purposely avoided dedicating whole chapters to them for three reasons:

1. There are plenty of resources that do an excellent job of examining spiritual disciplines.
2. Since we believe the purpose of spiritual disciplines is to create space for God to work within us, this book is more interested in looking at what happens to us on the inside when space is created. In other words, what are some of the everyday, real life outcomes of practicing the art of being?
3. Even though chapters aren't dedicated to specific disciplines, explanations on how to use specific disciplines are woven through the topics we cover.

The second section of this book focuses on the work of doing. Again, the topics we write about are not comprehensive, but they do adequately cover much of the work that naturally flows out of the art of being. They are also foundational principles that every youth worker should consider embracing. By "foundational," we mean that if you were to build a youth ministry from scratch, implementing these principles would be a good place to start. They are the *must do* for any youth worker. Interestingly, five of the six principles (the work of context, affection, contacting, resolution, and teaching) are about what youth workers should do personally to make disciples rather than what they should do programmatically. In most youth ministries, 80% of the focus and effort is given to programs, while only 20% is given to what youth workers do personally in the lives of kids. Yet we've discovered that 80% of the results in making disciples come from personal endeavors, not programming! Therefore, youth workers should always begin with what they can do personally to create an environment for making disciples. When they get the personal ministry stuff right, the program stuff almost always becomes second nature.

> **inside info**
>
> One chapter in *The Work of Doing* section is given to programming; but again, our approach is to speak more to the environment youth workers should create than to specific programming details. One of the future books mentioned in the introduction, *The Inside Out Youth Ministry*™, will take a comprehensive look at how to take an inside out approach to programming.

start painting

If you are a youth worker who is passionate about Christ's commission, reading this book should cause something inside of you to bubble to the surface. In other words, if you have a desire to make disciples among students at your core, when given the opportunity, that desire will surface. I hope this book is that opportunity for you! Let it give rise to the unique ArtWork God has placed inside of you, and let that ArtWork bubble up from the inside out. As you do, I believe you will discover some new ways Christ wants to shape you, as well as some new ways he wants to use you to shape teenagers.

Okay, it's time for art class. Let's start painting some inside out pictures.

inside out questions

1. Why do you think Jesus gave such special attention to making disciples? Why is it the main topic in his "graduation" commission?

2. What were Jesus' followers graduating *to* by accepting the challenge to make disciples?

3. What is your definition of "discipleship?" Is it the same as Jesus' definition? Does it include all three participles: "go," baptize" and "teach to obey?" Why or why not?

4. Describe the "art of being" in your own words?

5. Are you practicing the art of being?

6. Describe the "work of doing" in your own words?

7. Are you practicing the work of doing?

8. Which gets 80% of your attention: "programming" or "personal ministry" to teens? Do you need to make any changes? Why or why not?

9. What one thing would you like to see improve in your life and ministry because of reading this book?

part one:

• •

the art of BEING

"You must love the Lord your God with all your heart, all your soul, and all your mind." This is the first and greatest commandment.

Jesus Christ
Matthew 22:37-38

We have to remember that we look for solitude in order to grow there in love for God and in love for others. We do not go into the desert to escape people but to learn how to find them: we do not leave them in order to have nothing more to do with them, but to find out the way to do them the most good.

Thomas Merton
20th century Catholic mystic

Who looks outside, dreams; who looks inside, awakes.

Carl G. Jung
20th century Swiss psychiatrist

the art of
CHARACTER

by LeeTowns

What lies behind us and what lies before us are small matters compared to what lies within us.

Ralph Waldo Emerson

*G*od must be a cartoonist.

I know this statement sounds strange, but after almost two decades in youth ministry, I can't help but come to the conclusion that God is a cartoonist at heart. Here's why . . .

For a cartoonist, the characters he sketches are sincere expressions of himself—reflections of certain aspects of his personhood. This means that he labors to make the physical features of his drawings portray more than simple bodies. Each mark is measured so that the specific cartoon figures convey something deep from within the cartoonist's heart. To the average observer, cartoons might seem like just scribbles on paper; but to the cartoonist, they depict his soul.

Not as strange as you might of thought, huh?

Personally, I love cartoons and my favorite is *Calvin and Hobbes*. I especially enjoy Calvin. As a six year old, he is so naïve and innocent, yet there is a streetwise craftiness to him that I just love. In addition, his imagination and enthusiasm, which usually go totally unchecked, cause him to live life in complete abandonment—as if he is in the midst of a great adventure. Plus, he's just downright funny. When I read one of his escapades, I usually smile or laugh out loud, and I am always reminded of that audaciously daring kid that is deep within me.

When I reflect on *Calvin and Hobbes*, I also end up thinking about the first two youth ministry champions with whom I served; they were both actual cartoonists, and yet they were as opposite as two people could be. One was a robust, practical-joking, fun-loving, louder-than-life sort of guy. Students viewed him as the official overstuffed teddy bear of our youth group. The other fellow was a conservative, soft-spoken, organized professional, and although he wasn't outgoing or gregarious, students went to him whenever they needed guidance. Were these two colleagues different? You bet. Were each valuable to the Kingdom of God exactly the way God designed them? Absolutely!

> **inside info**
>
> Can you envision God at His drawing table? There he is measuring each line, sketching each personality, and forming each character trait. He's made revisions and corrections. Specific colors have been added and certain lines erased. Finally, he arrives at just the right character for just the right moment. He leans back and looks at his drawing with great delight. Can you hear him saying, "There she is. She's the one for this episode. Perfect!"?

In addition to the two cartoonists, God brought a wide variety of other people our way to enhance our ability to reach and love teens. A young college student on his way to becoming a marketing executive, a bi-racial couple, several nine-to-five blue-collar types, a stay-at-home mom with three children, a young married couple, and a college baseball player. What an amazing ensemble! On our own, none of us stood out as youth ministry superheroes. But together, God used us to accomplish super things. Our ministry reached into homes and lives in ways I never dreamed possible.

What made it possible? It's wasn't me. I was just a rookie, so the training and resources I provided were nothing to brag about. It wasn't the facilities. The church was nice, but again, it was nothing to brag about. And it wasn't our budget. We had some money, but not enough to add any bells or whistles. So what made the difference? It was the unique people God sketched into this particular ministry script. They had been carefully doodled by the Master Cartoonist long before I knew them. In fact, God had drawn each life in such a way that every one of us was able to impact particular students in ways no one else could. We all had a unique set of gifts and one-of-a-kind personalities. Yet, that wasn't all. God had also drawn, deep within each person, a unique character!

God's doodling

I hope one thought is becoming clear: cartoonists create character. Unlike movie producers, cartoonists don't pay a lot of attention to scripts, plot development, or storylines. Even more, while there is some consideration given to personality, it's not the item that gets the most attention. The top priority for a cartoonist is character development. With each sketch, the cartoonist attempts to reveal more about the internal nature and workings of the cartoon character than anything else. Sure, the story, the character's talents, and his or her personality are important, but nothing compares to character. In fact, follow a cartoon series long enough, and you'll be able to anticipate what a character will think, say, or do. The reason? Cartoonists spend years developing a character's character.

> *Oh yes, you shaped me first inside, then out; you formed me in my mother's womb.*
>
> Psalm 139:13
> The Message

It is likely you are reading this book to get a handle on what you should do in student ministry. In fact, when most people inquire about a paid or volunteer youth ministry position, they're usually handed some sort of job description. It might be printed in a 101-page manual or scribbled on a napkin, but the gist of practically every youth ministry job description is a list of the tasks for which you will be responsible. Although ministry tasks are important, don't be fooled, they don't matter most. The person you are on the inside is much more vital than the role you fill on the outside. Did you get that? When it comes to making disciples among teenagers, who you are at your core matters more than your position! Students respond to and are impacted by your character, regardless of whether you bring the pizza or teach the Bible. What's more, no person can be effective in making disciples without God sketching character within him. The bottom line is that character matters!

character defined

So what exactly does God doodle within the hearts of youth workers? How does he define character?

Even though each of us is a one-of-a-kind creation (something we'll discuss in a moment), there are common sketches and patterns God draws in all his followers. Just as Bill Watterson, the cartoonist who draws *Calvin and Hobbes*, created a boy who looks at life through young and innocent eyes, so too has Hank Ketcham, the artist who draws *Dennis the Menace*. Calvin and Dennis are not the same person, but they have similarities. Both are young, naïve, adventurous, and willing to express exactly what they feel—no matter who's listening.

In the same way, although every youth worker is unique, there are common sketches and patterns that God draws into all our lives. For one, we believe a relationship with Jesus Christ is essential for all people. Two, we love teenagers. Three, we believe adolescence is the best time to reach people with the good news of Christ. Four, we can no longer donate blood due to toxically high levels of pepperoni.

Okay, so the first three commonalties are true, and the fourth is probably not far from reality, but did you know we have even more in common than these basic qualities? There are actually nine inner qualities God wants to draw into the lives of every Christ-follower. As Paul wrote, "But when the Holy Spirit controls our lives, he will produce this kind of fruit in us: love, joy, peace, patience, kindness, goodness, faithfulness, gentleness, and self-control. Here there is no conflict with the law" (Galatians 5:22-23). God desires, through his Spirit, to sketch, shape, and color these nine traits inside every believer. Let's briefly examine each characteristic to get a better handle on how God is shaping us.

Love. Love is listed first and given more weight than any of the other qualities because all the others are defined by and flow out of love. What's more, when love is properly fleshed out, it is fundamentally a self-sacrificing action, not just an emotion. For example, "God so loved the world that he gave his only Son . . ." (John 3:16), "Love your neighbor as yourself . . ." (Leviticus 19:18), "Love your enemies! Pray for those who persecute you!" (Matthew 5:44), "Love covers a multitude of sins . . ." (1 Peter 4:8), and "Let us stop just saying we love each other; let us really show it by our actions" (1 John 3:18).

Joy. This is perhaps the most misunderstood quality on the list. Joy does not equal happiness. While happiness often flows from joy, it is possible to experience joy in the midst of great pain or sorrow, because joy transcends circumstances. Joy, which is a deep sense of satisfaction and fulfillment, comes from the confidence of knowing God is in control.

Peace. Like joy, peace also comes from confidence. However, while joy's confidence is in the present, peace is being confident about the future. Peace occurs when we trust God for outcomes that are yet to come and completely out of our control. "It is a tranquility of mind based on a right relationship to God . . . no matter what happens, you know everything between you and God is right."[5]

Patience. This word is pregnant with meaning. Its synonyms include tolerance, endurance, long suffering, stick-to-it-tiveness, and being slow to anger. It includes both waiting on God to complete his purposes and being patient with others.

Kindness. We live in a harsh world. Fists are shaken and expletives are yelled by people who lack patience, joy, and peace. In such a world, there is something refreshing about a person who surfaces kindness in a way that is tender and caring towards others. It's not that such an individual lacks conviction; instead, there is an inner strength to him that allows him to show kindness in spite of circumstances or how others treat him.

Goodness. Goodness is not just the ability to obey the law; it "refers to moral or spiritual excellence."[6] Goodness pushes a person past rightness into wholesomeness, and wholesome people are better equipped to impact others.

Faithfulness. Students need dependable people in their lives. They need trustworthy, loyal, steadfast, reliable adults who care and are consistently there for them. This is faithfulness—"the quality of keeping commitments in relationships."[7]

Gentleness. When I think of people who truly love students, there is one trait that seems most common—gentleness. "Gentleness is the opposite of 'selfish ambition.' Gentle people are not 'conceited, provoking and envying each other' (Galatians 5:26). Gentleness is an expression of humility, considering the needs and hurts of others before one's personal goals."[8] As I write this, dozens of images race through my mind of people expressing love for students through gentle conversations, expressions, and pats on the back.

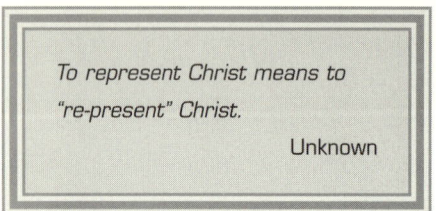

To represent Christ means to "re-present" Christ.
Unknown

Self-control. The final character trait the Spirit sketches into the lives of believers is self-control. "Self-control is the opposite of self-indulgence. Those who are Spirit-led will not indulge the sinful nature (Galatians 6:13) . . . They have the strength to say no to themselves and the desires of their sinful nature."[9] Self-control enables us to make the right decisions and take the right actions.

uniqueness of character

Even though the nine qualities of the fruit of the Holy Spirit are given to all believers, it is important to recognize that everyone is at a different stage of growth. This means certain traits will look different in different believers. As already mentioned, every Christ follower is a matchless, one-of-a-kind creation designed by the Master Cartoonist. Therefore, speaking hypothetically, if we compare two believers who are at the exact same place on the maturity scale, the way they would manifest the fruit of the Spirit would still be very different. This is because the way God sketches each one of us is distinct. Again, he is the Master Cartoonist and no two of his drawings are alike. In fact, God uniquely pre-designed our character.

*You made all the delicate, inner parts of my body
and knit me together in my mother's womb.
Thank you for making me so wonderfully complex!
Your workmanship is marvelous—and how well I know it.
You watched me as I was being formed in utter seclusion,
as I was woven together in the dark of the womb.
You saw me before I was born.
Every day of my life was recorded in your book.
Every moment was laid out
before a single day had passed (Psalm 139:13-16).*

The Hebrew word used in verse 13 for "inner parts" is *kilyah*, which literally means "kidneys." To Hebrew readers, kidneys were more than just vital organs; they were the seat of a person's emotions and moral character. Therefore, the Psalmist David is saying that the wonderful workmanship of God includes not only the formation of our inner physical parts, but also the creation of a unique character that is placed inside of us before we breathed our first breath. Even more, if every moment of our life is laid out before a single moment passes (verse 16), then the process of living, in a very real sense, is simply a means by which we discover and develop the character God has already placed within us. The picture I get is of Almighty God carefully measuring every line of my being, including my character, before I am born. He doesn't use an old, worn out blueprint that has been used thousands of times before; he starts fresh with a clean sheet of paper and a brand new idea. He designs me in a way that uniquely reveals his complex handiwork. I am his original, one-of-a-kind drawing, and throughout life, as I grow closer to Christ, the character that is inside emerges in a way that makes others marvel at his workmanship.

a doodle in development

Years ago, I had an artist friend who specialized in caricatures. I was interested in learning to draw cartoons, so I asked him for advice. What he said to me was simple, yet tremendously profound. "Start doodling!" He went on to say, "The more you draw a character, the better it gets, so you need to draw and draw and then draw some more." So that's what I did. I doodled during class. I doodled on napkins. I doodled in the steam on the shower walls. I doodled and doodled and doodled . . . everywhere and anywhere. Overtime, my little caricature started taking shape, and though I am not a published cartoonist yet, when my children ask me to draw a picture, I have a special creation I doodle just for them.

My cartoon is still a doodle in development. In fact, each time I draw it, I add something new or take something away. Sometimes, I make his facial expression a bit different. Other times, I change his hairstyle. Certain arcs may be enhanced or a particular shadow darkened, and with each modification, no matter how minor, I am refining his character. You might think the most important tool in this refinement process is my pencil. Or perhaps you'd guess my eraser. These are important, but believe it or not, my trashcan is just as vital. Why? Because in the height of creativity, my trashcan spills over with pictures I looked at and said, "This just isn't right." Although the discarded pile of paper might look like a tribute to failings, it actually represents an important tool in the refinement of my cartoon's character.

You and I experience a similar refining process. God, the Master Cartoonist, uses a variety of tools to shape us. At times, he uses his pencil to draw new, positive lines. Other times, God employs his eraser to make corrections or changes. He even uses his trashcan to discard the ugly and harmful sin we allow to creep into our lives. But in the hands of the Master Cartoonist, both the uplifting and the unpleasant become means of refinement. Both are used to create character. As Paul wrote, "We know that God causes everything to work together for the good of those who love God and are called according to his purpose for them" (Romans 8:28).

So let's look a bit more closely at the tools God uses to form our character . . .

pitfalls

God knows that every human—with the exception of his Son, the God-man Jesus—is sinful. He knows no one is perfect. Pause and re-read those two sentences again. Seriously, I'll give you time . . .

If these two sentences are true, then God knows you and I are going to fail. Even more, he anticipates it. He doesn't expect us to potentially stumble; he knows exactly where and when we will fall flat on our faces.

Depressed? Don't be. Without failure, grace is completely unnecessary. But praise God for his grace! When you and I sin, the process of confessing, repenting, and being forgiven brings about more than restoration, it is also a means God uses to create character. For instance, look at how Jesus responded to the woman taken in adultery. She made a ghastly, sinful decision, yet Jesus' response is beautiful and grace-filled. He looks her in the eyes and says, "Then neither do I condemn you. Go now and leave your life of sin" (John 8:11 NIV). Jesus transformed her horrific pitfall into an exercise in character refinement. He didn't condone or wink at sin; he threw it in the trash. He graciously forgave her and then freed her to leave her life of sin. While Satan tries to use sin to disqualify us, God can take the very thing that was meant to destroy us and through grace, use it to redeem our character. As proponents of Sonship theology state: "Cheer up, you are much worse than you think. But cheer up, God's grace is so much better than you can imagine."[10]

> **inside info**
>
> In my experience, past pitfalls often keep people from volunteering in youth ministry. When I started running background checks on volunteers, I received a flood of phone calls. Each person began the conversation with, "I don't think I can serve any longer." I'd ask why and each would share a past pitfall. Yet in almost every case, I discovered the pitfalls led to significant growth. What they viewed as a disqualifier had been used by God for transformation.
>
> Are you hesitant to serve in student ministry because of your past? Remember, God often uses our past, even our past mistakes, to prepare us for future ministry.

problems

God also uses problems to shape character. Inevitably, things come into our lives that are not the results of our decisions or actions; they are just dilemmas. While no one is quick to embrace difficulty, problems can be used by God to chisel away things that would keep our character from fully emerging. For instance, several volunteers in my ministry come from broken homes. They are not responsible for the break up of their parents, and none of them would have purposely chosen to have gone through this experience as a child. However, God has used their experiences to refine their characters and open up opportunities that make them uniquely suited to help students who face similar circumstances. So even something as difficult and painful as divorce can be used "for the good of those who love God and are called according to his purposes" (Romans 8:28).

> A gem cannot be polished without friction, nor people perfected without trails.
>
> Chinese proverb

pain

Another reality we cannot escape is that, at times, life hurts. Pitfalls and problems cause pain, but they are not the only contributors. Sickness, the death of a loved one, disappointment, and unmet dreams all sting. Nevertheless, in the midst of hardship, God is still sketching and using life's pain to produce character. God does not carelessly allow pain to enter our lives; instead, he deliberately brings about specific events to form the character he wants us to develop. Although diffi-

> We can rejoice, too, when we run into problems and trials, for we know that they are good for us—they help us learn to endure. And endurance develops strength of character in us, and character strengthens our confident expectation of salvation. And this expectation will not disappoint us. For we know how dearly God loves us, because he has given us the Holy Spirit to fill our hearts with his love.
>
> Romans 5:3-5

cult, we cannot allow pain to sideline or disqualify us. Rather, we must trust God to use even the most excruciating circumstances to develop the inward traits that only pain can produce.

practices

Most believers acknowledge that spiritual practices like devotions, prayer, journaling, fasting, tithing, and church involvement help build character. However, many get stuck in the trap of viewing these practices as a means of scoring brownie points with God. That's not their purpose at all. Practicing spiritual disciplines, no matter how committed we are to them, will not cause God to love or accept us any more than he already does. Remember, he sent his Son to die for us while we were still sinners (Romans 5:8); how can he love us more than that? The purpose of spiritual disciplines is to help us focus on God so that we are more aware of what he is doing and wants to do inside of us.

process

Life is happening all around us. We continually face circumstances that are painful, hard, and uncomfortable, as well as others that are delightful, energizing, and fun. Each circumstance serves in our journey as a means of character development because every step, whether difficult or easy, has been intentionally designed by God. Therefore, one of the best ways to experience God scribbling his character on our hearts is to simply realize that all of life is spiritual. Our careers, social life, family life, finances, community involvement, church involvement, spiritual disciplines, and physical life are all spiritual, and God can use each to refine our character.

> *Character cannot be developed in ease and quiet. Only through experience of trial and suffering can the soul be strengthened, vision cleared, ambition inspired, and success achieved.*
>
> Helen Keller
> American blind and deaf writer/lecturer

you are a unique caricature

Earlier, I described my first ministry team as a group of people who were able to make disciples among a wide variety of students. One student, however, was more difficult than most. He was a bit of an outcast who struggled through middle school and early high school, often feeling lonely and left out. You can imagine how he felt when I, as the youth pastor, would challenge the group each week to make a difference on their campuses. He'd think, "Me, make a difference? Yeah, right!" The challenge not only overwhelmed him, it made him feel more disconnected from God and our group.

One day, one of our volunteers noticed him messing with a pile of papers. When the volunteer asked about the papers, he discovered this student had created an animation book. The book was hundreds of pages and he had drawn a caricature on each page. The cartoon was slightly different on every page so that when it was flipped through rapidly, the character was in full motion. Unbeknownst to anyone on our team, this young man was a budding cartoonist!

> Fame is vapor, popularity an accident, riches take wing, and only character endures.
>
> Horace Greeley
> 19th century
> New York newspaper editor

I bet you already know which volunteer connected with this fellow. You are absolutely right—one of our cartoonists. God, in his divine sovereignty, had brought together a caring adult who wanted to serve students and a certain teenager who needed an adult just like him. As they connected, this "loner" began to blossom. He grew closer to Christ and even started to believe he could make a difference in the lives of others. Was it just a coincidence that these two cartoonists hooked up? I think not.

In the same way, God, in his divine sovereignty, has sketched you into a specific youth ministry episode to serve certain teenagers who need a caring adult just like you. Coincidence? I think not. He has been shaping your character for years—preparing you with his pencil, eraser, and even his trashcan. You are ready, inside and out, to make disciples among teenagers. So get to it! Be the character you were created to be and watch what God does in and through you.

inside out questions

1. In this chapter, "character" was defined by the fruit of the Spirit. Which aspects of the fruit of the Spirit are most fully developed in your life and which still need to grow?

Love	Goodness
Joy	Faithfulness
Peace	Gentleness
Patience	Self-control
Kindness	

2. What can you do to create an environment in your life that is conducive to seeing God grow the fruit of the Spirit in you?

3. How has God used the following tools to form your character? Be as specific as possible.

Pitfalls	Practices
Problems	Process
Pain	

3. What is unique about your character? What are some of the one-of-a-kind traits God has sketched into your life?

4. How can God use the uniqueness of your character to help you make disciples among teenagers?

the art of BALANCE

by Melinda Lankford

Balance isn't either/or, it's and.

Stephen Covey

Ever feel overwhelmed trying to balance life and ministry? Me too!

A frequent prayer of mine goes something like this, "Help! I'm out of control!" Right from the start, I confess I'm no expert on the topic of balance. What I am, however, is someone who has served in youth ministry for more than eleven years while transitioning through the following life stages: working full-time, planning a wedding, being a newlywed, having children, and being a stay-at-home mom. I've frequently wanted to throw in the towel, and on other occasions, I've smugly thought I've had it all together. Through it all, God has graciously helped me learn a few lessons about inside out balance.

questions, questions, questions

Let's start by answering a few questions that will help us approach the topic of balance from a similar starting point.

are you in or out?

You probably wouldn't be reading this book if you didn't want to work with youth. Yet, before going any further, be sure you can answer the "in or out" question with a definite "I'M IN!" If you're not in, students know. You can't hide your true intentions from them, so don't try. If your heart isn't really into youth ministry, go ahead and transition out. Serve in your area of passion and do so with no worries—the Lord will provide someone else to serve students.

why strive for balance?

Do you want to stay in youth ministry for the long haul? Do you value sanity? Balance is required for both. But more importantly, learning the art of balance adds some great benefits to life. For instance, balance enhances our relationship with Christ. If my life is a chaotic whirlwind, my connection with God usually gets short-circuited. Lack of connection eventually leads to more chaos, less focus, and I usually do something I regret. Practicing the art of balance helps me connect consistently with Christ.

The art of balance also benefits family and friends. At times, my family and friends have been unnecessarily neglected because of my unbalanced approach to youth ministry. I could give dozens of heart-tugging examples, but just take my word for it, neglect isn't pretty.

When we practice balance, the students we serve also benefit. Working in youth ministry for so long has allowed me to serve alongside volunteers who were my former students. Remarkably, some have said to me, "Thanks for modeling a full, yet balanced life. Because of your example, I know I can be a loving wife, a caring mom, and an active follower of Christ." As you can imagine, these comments inspire me to pursue balance.

what exactly is balance?

Ever tried juggling? It's not too difficult. With a good teacher and a bit of practice, you'll be juggling in just a few days. Although most novices can juggle three objects at a time, being able to keep four, five, or six items in the air at once takes years of practice to master.

Ever waited tables in a restaurant? This isn't too difficult either. Sure, you must keep track of multiple orders, refill water glasses, and plaster a smile on your face; but again, with a good trainer and a bit of practice, you'll be capable of waiting on four or five tables simultaneously.

Now imagine a juggling waiter! Can you envision him picking up an order in the kitchen? Instead of balancing four or five dishes on a tray, he flips on some circus music, picks up each plate, and begins tossing them five or six feet into the air. Since he's an excellent juggler, the plates arrive at the correct tables unbroken, but broccoli stalks land in people's drinks and a rack of ribs almost takes a kid's head off. The customers are served, but they are not served well. The reason? The waiter was never in control. While one or two plates were in his hands, the others where soaring through the air.

When a youth worker tries to juggle life, work, marriage, family, finances, friends, and ministry, his "customers" might get served, but they're probably not served well because he's not in control. Like good waiters, youth workers must learn to take the items on their "tray" and move each one around until they are able to balance those items. This allows them to see exactly what is on their tray and gives them a feel for how much they can carry. That's a portrait of balance!

> **inside info**
>
> The word "control" arouses good and bad emotions. Depending on the context, it can mean being organized, restrained, and well managed, or it can indicate someone is commanding, dictating, and power hungry. In our context, control means managing well the resources God gives us. It refers to good stewardship.

Let's take a look at a real life example. Nine years ago, I discovered I was completely out of control in what I was eating. After years of struggling with food and weight, I found, through a 12-step program, that I was a compulsive overeater. Finally admitting I had a problem was devastating. Even more heartbreaking, however, was realizing my uncontrollable eating tendencies were seeping into other areas of my life and causing havoc.

The good news is that my lack of balance slowly morphed into balance as I listened and learned from others who struggled with the same disorder. I started developing a picture of what life could be like if I controlled my eating instead of letting my eating control me. During the past nine years, for the most part, I've been in control. Before you give me a standing ovation, you should know that the road has been bumpy. I'd rather not live with the discipline of a 12-step program, recurring meetings, and a sponsor, but I've come to realize that I need structure and accountability.

In the same way, balancing youth ministry with the rest of life can be a bumpy road. In fact, if you'd take a random survey of youth workers, many would indicate their lives are too chaotic. But have faith; your picture can evolve just like mine! With a little encouragement and accountability, you'll find the path.

inside out balance

It is possible to balance youth ministry with real life. As already stated, I've served in youth ministry as a single woman working full-time, as a woman planning a wedding while working full-time, as a wife working full-time, and now as a stay-at-home wife and mother. So believe me when I tell you that it can be done! Remember, you said, "I'm in," so let's figure out how you can stay in. The key, of course, is making sure you're balanced inside and out. Since balance on the inside leads to balance on the outside, we will start by looking at how we can be more balanced people and then discuss how to balance our activities better. Please realize, the four suggestions given here are not quick-fixes, but like a 12-step program, they should provide a good structure on which you can build an overall balanced plan.

suggestion one: predetermine spiritual meals

It took me 26 years to discover I needed to predetermine what I was going to physically eat; it took me even longer to discover how to do it spiritually. Yet, if I want to make disciples among teenagers by investing in them spiritually, I must be able to properly feed myself first. How does spiritual nourishment happen? For me, it requires prioritizing and planning.

Prioritizing me. "You need to prioritize you!" The first time I heard this in a 12-step meeting, I almost walked out. How offensive! What about having a servant's heart and placing someone else's needs ahead of mine? Yet after some reflection, I realized there is truth in this statement. In Matthew 22:39, Jesus commands us to love our neighbors as ourselves. How can we follow this command if we ignore the second half of it? If we are to love others well, we must also love ourselves well. A great example of someone who loves himself properly is Jesus. According to Philippians 2, he emptied himself for our sake. But think about it, before emptying himself, he had to have something to give. Since he was "the very nature of God" (verse 6), he was capable of "making himself nothing" (verse 7), "humbling himself" (verse 8), and giving himself up for us. In the same way, if we are to serve others, we must have something to give, and our "something" is Christ. Since we can only experience more of Christ by connecting more with him, we need to prioritize him. Do you see what I'm getting at? By prioritizing myself, I am actually prioritizing Jesus in my life. By doing this, I am better prepared to make disciples among teenagers.

Planning for me. Once we choose to prioritize our relationship with Christ, the natural next step to being a balanced person on the inside is the development of a solid plan. I have never been good at daily devotions. I know—you're terribly disappointed in me; well, so am I, but improvement only occurs when we are honest with ourselves. I can be an incredibly disciplined person with schoolwork, house cleaning, or a food plan; yet, I often drop the ball when it comes to my time with God. Why? Because I have no plan. Without structure supporting my daily quiet times, they just don't happen. I felt guilty for years before I finally figured out that being accountable in a Bible Study or developing a one-on-one relationship where someone is counting on me is my key to staying consistent in my personal time with God. This is how I plan for me. Since this discovery, I make sure I am always somehow accountable to someone. I know myself; if I don't plan, it won't happen.

What about you? What's your plan? Are you prioritizing your walk with Christ, or do you just eat spiritual junk food on the run? My eating disorder taught me the importance of predetermining my physical meals through prioritizing and planning, but it has also helped me realize that this approach is even more important spiritually.

suggestion two: pose inside out questions

As you've probably noticed, I ask a lot of questions. Questions force us to be intentional. The questions I asked earlier dealt broadly with the concept of balance, but the following questions focus more on what's going on inside of you. They are good self-check questions to keep handy when you are considering what your spiritual meal plan should include.

Am I spiritually full? This question does not ask, "Do we have all of God that we need"; it asks, "Are we open to God doing whatever He wants in our lives?" Are you ready for him to shape you at your core—no matter what? If you cannot answer yes, then you should probably reevaluate your spiritual meals. Remember, spending time alone with Christ does not make us spiritual; it prepares us to be spiritual. Spirituality is reflected in how we live and in our disciple-making lifestyle, so our planned times with God should be designed to prepare us to be Christ-like. If you're not being prepared for Christ-like living, consider what's missing. Talk to a trusted friend. Journal your thoughts. Make sure the meals you plan fill you.

Am I a spiritual glutton? Spiritual meal plans shouldn't just prepare us for what God wants to do in us; they should empower us for what God wants to do through us. Again, spirituality is fleshed out in real life, which means truly spiritual people serve others. If you feed on spiritual truths, yet never invest in others, you're a glutton.

Am I spiritually dehydrated? Since youth ministry is like a marathon, we often lose essential fluids and minerals and need to stop at spiritual "fluid stations" along the race path. These breaks are different from our prioritized meals; they just pop up periodically. For instance, a few months after my husband and I moved, our friends took us to an outdoor concert where the majority of the three hours were spent under the stars in participatory worship. I had no idea how spiritually thirsty I was until about 15 minutes into the concert when I began to weep and thank the Lord for the opportunity to simply worship Him—not do something for him, but simply worship him. I'd been so busy running the race that I was dehydrated. No matter how much prioritizing and planning we do, we'll still experience dry times, and God, in his grace, provides fluid stations along the journey at just the right time and place. Look for these and be sure to stop.

suggestion three: prioritize family

Youth ministry is a BLAST! What other ministry gives opportunities to participate in the absolutely bizarre (e.g. shooting SPAM® from a balloon launcher or bobbing for candy bars in oatmeal), embrace carefree fun (e.g. snow boarding, jet skiing, etc.), authentically worship God, and use our gifts to make disciples among teenagers? All these elements and more can even take place during a single weekend retreat! But youth ministry also takes tons of time and energy. Working with teenagers is demanding, and if you are not careful, you'll find yourself neglecting other important areas of life like marriage and family to do youth ministry well. How do youth workers balance so many opportunities and relationships?

Spouse. If you are married, youth ministry WILL drain your relationship with your spouse if you let it. However, Chris and I have found we don't feel drained if we prioritize our marriage. We have two tips to pass on that have worked well for us. (By the way, Chris and I are not gifted in the art of saying "no," so our tendency is to over-commit. Since we are not "naturally balanced," we've developed some strict boundaries.)

First, when Chris and I got married, someone recommended that we maintain a sacred date night, and we have dutifully followed this practice our entire marriage. No matter how busy our lives and ministry get, we set aside one night a week to talk and play together. This tradition has saved our marriage and created some of our best memories. The key is, we do it—no matter how busy we are, whether we have money or not, and even if we have to leave a sick child with a babysitter. It's that important!

Second, we plan regular getaways just for us. For instance, we attend an annual marriage retreat that gives us an opportunity to evaluate our marriage,

---

outward action

If your spouse doesn't serve in youth ministry, prioritizing your marriage is extremely crucial since youth ministry will take you away from time to time. Therefore, be sure to communicate two things:

- Your spouse is your greatest priority—use both words and actions to communicate this truth.
- Youth ministry is also a priority—let your spouse know what youth ministry will require by defining time commitments and nights out.

gain a few relational tips, and just spend time reconnecting. This weekend has become a highlight for us every year.

Children. Because of the success of our personal date nights, we added date nights with our two daughters to our family rituals as well. The girls get to pick where we go and always get dessert at the end of the evening. Chris and I are also not allowed to use our cell phones while on these dates (a rule established by our six-year-old), and we must talk with the girls, not just with one another. I'm not boasting about our parenting skills, I'm just pointing out how important our kids are to us. We love them and must prioritize time with them so they feel important and special. Jessalyn likes to say, "My Mommy and Daddy, no one else's," and she's right! Ministry can take over our lives, so Chris and I set family time that belongs to "no one else" but our kids.

Do you have children? What ways do you let them know your family takes priority status? Make sure you find your own special ways to let your children know that you are "no one else's."

Combining family and students. Once you're clear about prioritizing marriage and family, you're ready to discover the magic of combining family and ministry. This approach has been a key to our longevity in youth ministry since finding time to interact with students outside of youth group becomes difficult once you start a family of your own. Before children, Chris and I had the freedom to attend sporting events or school musicals. But once we had children, the number of student events we could go to dropped significantly. I thought my days of meaningful contacting were over until I decided to swing by a soccer game with my 3-year-old. Wow, what a place to take her! She had a blast, and the teenagers were thrilled to have a little cheerleader on the sidelines. Over the

> **inside info**
>
> The examples in this chapter for prioritizing important relationships revolve around spouses and kids. If you aren't married or don't have children, you still have significant relationships. Be sure to prioritize them! Use the ideas here to invest in the people who are important to you such as parents, extended family, a fiancé, and close friends.

years, I've discovered this "drop by" strategy is an awesome way to connect with teenagers; students enjoy seeing my kids and me, and we love seeing them.

So, how do I do this? I already shared my first "drop by" experience. After that little success, I started doing lunch with girls in my small group. This gives me a chance to connect with them outside the church setting and an excuse to get my two little ones out of the house. None of the teenagers seem to mind, even though our conversations are occasionally interrupted by little voices asking for drinks or help cutting their chicken strips. My husband also uses the "drop by" strategy to take our kids with him to all kinds of student activities. Our girls see this time as a daddy date, while students are thrilled to have Chris at their event. Chris and I have even budgeted "ministry money" so we have cash on hand to grab a bite to eat with students or attend an event without creating a budget battle between us.

There is another strategy we use that is even more powerful than the "drop by"; we let students "drop in" at our home. Chris and I see our home as a gift from God and opening up this gift to students brings us great joy. When teens are comfortable hanging out at our house, we know they are getting comfortable with us. What makes this strategy so powerful is all the added bonuses that accompany it. For example, it gives teens a glimpse at how a Christian family interacts—something many of them do not experience at home. Our family isn't perfect, but because Christ is such a part of who we are, there is a lot of love, support, encouragement, and forgiveness expressed. Seeing Christ-like values fleshed out in a family is transformational. It also gives our children a chance to see what making disciples looks like in the real world, and this is an invaluable education for them. For instance, my small group has been over for sleepovers, ice cream socials, movie-

> **inside info**
>
> If you are single, inviting teenagers over to your house or apartment might be an issue. Be sure to clear everything with parents, the youth ministry point person, and any other necessary church authority before handing out invitations.

making nights, and nights of worship and testimony, and my daughters have been involved in all of them. I've even recruited teenage girls to dress as Disney Princesses, do face painting, and serve cake at my daughter's birthday parties. The memories made for both the teenagers and my children are priceless! But more importantly, my daughters are seeing and hearing me share Jesus with others. They're seeing us use our house and family as a tool for making disciples of Jesus Christ among teenagers!

If you're like me, this sounds exciting but also overwhelming. You want to use your home as a ministry tool, but you also need your space. Before waving that "I like my space" flag, know that I'm an introverted-extrovert. In other words, everybody thinks I run on energy from the crowd, but I actually crave alone time. Therefore, I'm not suggesting you put a note in the youth ministry newsletter that says, "Drop by any time." Instead, structure "drop by" times. Perhaps you can designate one night a week when students know they can pop in on your family. Or maybe you can host a monthly game night at your home. Whatever you decide, use the time to strengthen relationships with teens and your family. Remember, the real bonus of the "drop in" strategy is that you can connect with students while hanging out with your family.

> **inside info**
>
> The "drop in" strategy guarantees you will have more stains on your carpet and that your furniture will wear out faster. Yet remember, the relationships you build with students will be deeper and more valuable!

Hopefully you're getting the picture—finding balance between family and ministry doesn't always mean separating the two. Yes, family needs to be prioritized, but there are ways to combine both. Moreover, the benefits for both students and your family can be a clear demonstration of your disciple-making priorities.

suggestion four: purposeful ministry

After predetermining your spiritual meals, posing inside out questions, and prioritizing family, the final tip is to ensure you are purposeful in ministry. Designing your ministry approach around who you are, the time you have to give, and the boundaries you have set will guarantee that what you do to make disciples among teenagers is strategic and effective.

Who are you? Being honest with yourself about who you are—your strengths, weaknesses, talents, and flaws—is one of the starting points of purposeful ministry. Why did God choose you to do this work? How and where does he want to use you? What does he want to do in you through your involvement in youth ministry? Being purposeful in ministry requires you to be clear about who you are and what you believe God is asking you to do.

How much time can you give? Each of us only has so much time to give to youth ministry, so making the most of it is important. When I evaluate the time I give to youth ministry, I sometimes realize I'm not being nearly as effective as I'd like to be and am actually wasting time. Kent Julian, the general editor of this book, helps his volunteers make the most of their time by challenging them to divide up their weekly five-hour commitment to youth ministry as follows: the first hour should go to praying for students, the second hour to building intentional relationships with students, and the remaining three hours to preparing and participating in programs. This approach helps his volunteers invest their time wisely.

Would this work for you? If so, then use it. If not, what would? Think this through. Also, consider how much time you currently commit to youth ministry. Can you give more? Do you need to give less? What requirements are being placed on you? Is this the best use of your time and talents? By structuring your time commitment, you create a ministry that is both purposeful and measurable.

Where are your fence posts? Those who want to be purposeful in ministry also establish boundaries to protect themselves and to keep ministry commitments from being preyed upon by other demands. I like to think of boundaries as fence posts that keep me from wandering off into dangerous areas while still giving me complete of freedom inside their boarders. Establishing strong fence posts is important because our families, churches, and students are counting on us to be people of integrity and commitment. Proper boundaries allow us to deliver on these expectations.

For instance, a male youth worker friend of mine has protected his

> **inside info**
>
> "Trying to balance family and ministry often pits one against the other—family on one side of the teeter-totter and ministry on the other. When one is up, the other is down...
>
> Family and ministry need to move to the center where we can live in a shared, radical middle, navigating life's ups and downs. Some of the ways we've attempted to live in this 'radical middle' have come about by asking questions such as these...
>
> - Does my family see my ministry role as 'my calling' or 'our calling'?
> - What would it look like for our whole family to be praying for our ministry?
> - Do I champion my spouse's gifts and passions?
> - Does he or she share my calling for ministry in some way?
> - Am I willing to walk away from a ministry role if our calling as a couple or family doesn't line up?
> - Are we comparing ourselves to other families?
> - Do we have unrealistic expectations?"
>
> Dave Livermore and Steve Argue taken from "Jesus-style Youth Ministry: Focus Through The Family," *GROUP Magazine*, May-June 2005, 30.

family and reputation by setting a boundary that prohibits him from ever being alone with someone of the opposite sex. He never allows himself to be in a room or an automobile one-on-one with a female—either a student or an adult. It's his way of protecting his relationship with his wife and children from unnecessary misunderstandings, rumors, and mistakes. Has this been inconvenient at times? You bet! Yet, the inconvenience is a small price to pay to protect his reputation and family.

Boundaries also work by keeping other obligations from crowding out our youth ministry commitments. When I worked outside the home, I made a point of letting my supervisor know that I would need to leave early on Tuesday nights for high school youth group. Once my supervisor knew Tuesday nights were out, he honored my commitment. In fact, he even went so far as to poke his nose in my office on Tuesday nights to give me "Isn't this the night you have church?" reminders. Communicate your boundaries upfront with employers, family members, and anyone else who depends on you; it will save you a lot of headaches and hard decisions later.

Boundaries also mean saying "no" to some opportunities, so you can say "yes" to youth ministry. At one time, I served as a deaconess and youth worker simultaneously. I would drag myself into Saturday morning deaconess meetings after Friday night youth activities—wondering what I was doing. My passion was not in being a deaconess, but I felt required to serve since I'd been asked. It finally dawned on me that God probably wanted to use a person in the deaconess role who had a bit more passion for the position, so I stepped down. I was able to give more time and energy to making disciples among teenagers, and it opened the door for someone more qualified to be a deaconess.

Sometimes saying "no" even comes in the area of youth ministry itself. When I am leading a small group, I try to give extra time to building relationships with the girls in my group. This means saying "no" to things like running PowerPoint or being on the worship team so I can be free to hang out with my students. Think carefully about what you say "yes" to because every "yes" is usually a "no" to something else.

help! i'm out of balance

I laughed when I was asked to write this chapter. "Balance? Are you kidding? I'm more of a juggler than a balancer!" But when I thought about it, I realized that yes, I do tend to juggle too much, but I've come a long way and am getting much better at balancing. I now know what balance looks like, what it takes to stay balanced, and how to get back in balance when I've mistakenly reverted to my old juggling routines.

So, if you feel like you are having trouble keeping all the plates in the air, don't panic. In fact, be encouraged because now you have a few ideas about how to catch those plates and balance them on your tray. Apply some of the suggestions in this chapter, and you'll be on your way to being balanced. Above all else, remember that balance is not just something you attain, but something you maintain. Your goal is to successfully invest yourself in the big roles God has called you to play—spouse, parent, professional, and youth worker; so live like a good waiter who has learned to make constant adjustments to his tray. Soon, balance will not only be your dream, it will be your reality!

inside out questions

1. Do you feel like you balance or juggle responsibilities?

2. Why is striving for balance in life so important if you want to make disciples of Jesus Christ among teenagers?

3. What do you do to prioritize and plan spiritual meals for yourself? Is there anything you can do to improve in this area?

4. Do any of the following statements currently describe you? Why?

    - I am spiritually full.
    - I am a spiritual glutton.
    - I am spiritually dehydrated.

5. How do you prioritize significant relationships in your life—such as with your spouse, children, extended family, work associates, and the teenagers you serve? Answer as specifically as possible.

6. Were the "drop by" and "drop in" strategies appealing to you? If so, how could you implement these strategies to combine family and ministry?

7. What boundaries have you set in your life regarding youth ministry? Are they helping you make disciples of Jesus Christ among students? Do you need to set any other boundaries?

the art of CONFIDENCE

by Kent Julian

If we did all the things we are capable of doing, we would literally astound ourselves.

Thomas A. Edison

Why did you get into youth ministry?

For me, it was because a junior high basketball coach and a volunteer youth worker had confidence in me.

heroes

In elementary school, I was a loser and I knew it. It's not like I was depressed or unhappy; I was one of those nice kids that got along with everyone. However, I did struggle. Academically, I had a significant speech impediment, and by the time I reached third grade, my teacher had to ask my parents how I passed the previous grades without being able to read. Simply put, I wasn't the "sharpest tack in the box." Physically, I wasn't much to look at either. I was short, chubby, wore Tough Skin Jeans, and had brown, square-framed glasses. But what was most difficult for me was my lack of athletic ability. I loved sports, but my arms and legs never supported that passion. Let's just say when it came time to choose kickball teams; I prayed not to be picked last. That way, at least I knew I wasn't the biggest loser on the playground.

When I hit junior high, I grew—so fast, in fact, that by the beginning of eighth grade, I was almost as tall as I am now. Along with this growth spurt came some athletic ability, not a lot, but enough that I decided to tryout for the junior high basketball team in seventh grade. Jim Vaught, the junior high coach, kept 15 players that year. When he met with me, he told me I was the last person to make the team. The conversation wasn't a "aren't you lucky" speech, but more of an "I believe in you" chat. He told me I probably wouldn't see a ton of playing time, but if I worked hard, next year could be a different story. To be honest, I wasn't really listening; I was just thrilled to make the team. In my mind, I'd never be a real athlete, so just being associated with jocks was an improvement from my perennial loser status. I still wasn't confident, but at least now, I could fake like I was.

> *Think you can or think you can't; either way you're right.*
>
> Henry Ford
> founder of Ford Motor Company

During the season, I made a major personal mistake; something that to this day I am still ashamed of having done. The details aren't necessary, just know it was *major*. And not only was the sin major, so was the context. I attended a small Christian school, both my parents taught at the school, and Mr. Vaught was not only the junior high basketball coach, but he was also my seventh grade math teacher and junior high principal. When Mr. Vaught called me into his office to confront me about my alleged transgression, I had no idea I had been caught. When he dropped the bomb, I was devastated. The sin was bad enough, but at that moment, I realized my parents, my teachers, and a basketball coach who believed in me were all disappointed in me. All the confidence that had been budding within this fragile seventh grader was cut short.

Or was it?

Mr. Vaught helped turn a potentially devastating situation into a positive watershed moment in my life. He was firm. He was even disappointed. Yet he still believed in me. I could sense it. I saw it in his eyes and heard it in his voice. Even in the midst of saying the hard things, I knew he believed I was a special kid with a special future. He clearly communicated that my tomorrow didn't need to be created from my yesterday; that my future was still in the future. He challenged me to own up to my sin, seek forgiveness, learn from it, and move on. A number of years later, I named the lesson he taught me. I call it *living life with my back to the past*. It means I recognize my past, both the good and the bad, take time to learn and grow from it, and then I move on. I refuse to campout in my history or walk backwards through life keeping my eyes glued to what has been. I choose to face the future and walk with my eyes forward. This powerful principle, which I use daily, was learned in the midst of adolescence through the tutelage of a junior high basketball coach.

> Confidence is contagious. So is lack of confidence.
>
> Vince Lombardi
> head coach of the Green Bay Packers
> and winner of the first 2 Super Bowls

At the end of the season, Mr. Vaught pulled me aside for another chat. The incident had happened only a month or so earlier, so I had been avoiding coach. I'd see him in class and at basketball practice, but I always kept my distance. So at first, when he wanted to talk, I was afraid he was going to rehash my mistake. Instead, all he said was, "Kent, I think you could get significant playing time next year if you work hard this summer. I really do!" When next year rolled around, not only was I starting, I led the team in scoring. At the awards ceremony, Mr. Vaught stood in front of a packed gym and said something along these lines: "I want to recognize Kent Julian. Last year, he was the last person picked for the team. This summer, he dedicated himself to practicing four to five hours a day. He played lunchtime games with business men at a local Rec. Center; he figured if he could play against grown men, seventh and eighth graders wouldn't be too difficult. Because of his effort, he was our leading scorer and most valuable player."

Nice words, huh? Almost thirty years later, I have a hard time writing them without getting choked up. But honestly, Jim Vaught left one detail out. I accomplished those things because he believed in me. If he had handled my watershed moment differently, those words would have never been uttered, at least not about me. My relationship with Jim Vaught—a man who saw me at my worst, yet chose to believe in my best—was what inspired me. Because he believed in me, I started to believe. And it didn't just affect my basketball skills, confidence spilled over into other areas of life as well.

Dan Glaze also helped steer me in the right direction during another watershed moment in my life. Dan was the volunteer youth leader at the church I started attending in eighth grade. The moment I met Dan, I liked him, and throughout high school, we did so much together that he literally became one of my best friends.

> Failure is the opportunity to begin again more intelligently.
>
> Henry Ford
> founder of the Ford Motor Company

During my junior year, a couple of events took place that left a bad taste in my mouth for God and Christianity. Looking back, these incidents were pretty typical "owning your faith" kind of stuff that occurs in the lives of lots of teenagers. For me, however, I ended up deciding not to own my faith, and even though I liked Dan, I become less and less pro-Dan because of his strong belief in Christ. We still hung out, and I still attended church, I was just distant. Plus, I started making trouble. During youth group, I purposely pushed the envelope, which meant Dan had to ask me to leave the room at least once a month. Like Jim Vaught, Dan handled these confrontations firmly but graciously. No matter how hard I tried, I could never push Dan around, and I was just as unsuccessful in making him lose his cool. I knew my behavior disappointed him, he told me so for goodness sake, but I also knew he believed in me. Why? Because, again, he told me so.

After graduation, my journey away from God continued. I didn't do anything too crazy, but my heart continued to shrink. Christianity seemed irrelevant, especially when I looked at other Christians. I didn't want to be like any of them . . . except Dan. He was different, so I stayed in touch with him. I was curious about why he was so whole-heartedly sold on Christ when everyone else seemed to just "do" Christianity. During these turbulent years, he was my lifeline. If God was worth following, I knew I could discover the reasons by staying in touch with Dan.

Again, without going into all the details, around the age of twenty, God called me back to himself and used Dan as the major player. What's more, when I sensed God wanted me to work full-time with students, I talked with Dan. I remember standing in the church parking lot around midnight and hearing him say, "Kent, I've been doing youth ministry for fifteen years, and if I had to do it all over again, and you were the only guy who ended up following Christ, I'd do it." He went on to say he was more excited about my relationship with Christ than whether or not I was going into youth ministry. According to him, I would be successful in whatever I pursued, but he was more concerned that I'd succeed in following Christ. This experience with Dan, like the one with Jim Vaught, boosted my confidence. If he could believe in me, I could too.

I've stayed in touch with both Jim and Dan. Both are heroes of mine. The gifts they gave me—friendship, grace, firmness, laughter, and an image of what true followers of Christ should look like—will stay with me for life. But as I've indicated throughout both stories, the greatest gift they gave me was confidence. Both men were confident in God and what he wanted to do through them, and their confidence seeped into me. It's been a key feature in my life and ministry. I don't say this arrogantly, but thankfully, as this chapter will reflect.

something's wrong

The art of confidence isn't seen much in youth ministry today. Authenticity . . . sometimes. Brokenness . . . occasionally. Humbleness . . . every now and them. But confidence?

Don't misunderstand—authenticity, brokenness, and humility are traits to which we should aspire. I'm just wondering why confidence isn't a topic of conversation or demonstrated more. I've been in youth ministry for two decades and have had a front row seat to its evolution.

> *Pessimism kills the instinct that urges men to struggle against poverty, ignorance and crime, and dries up all the fountains of joy in the world.*
>
> Helen Keller
> American blind and deaf
> writer/lecturer

Some changes have been fantastic: technological advances, the emphasis on worship, an explosion of small groups, student-to-student ministries, the search for true community, and of course, Starbucks (just had to throw this last one in). Yet, some changes have been less than stellar. For instance, sarcasm, cynicism, and outright negativity seem to be the norm among many youth workers today, and I remember a time when they weren't. It's as if in our attempt to be real and authentic, the scales have been tipped too much. Discussion almost always revolves around authentic hurt, real pain, genuine brokenness, and total depravity. This isn't necessarily bad; however, when struggles and battle wounds get all the headlines, successes and victories are relegated to the back page. When this happens, something's out of whack.

true confidence

Perhaps these comments raise red flags in your mind because you remember when practically every youth ministry book or curriculum revolved around helping teens develop healthy self-images. Pop psychology ruled, and you're not interested in going back to those days. Well, neither am I. Attempting to build confidence by ignoring sin and using gimmicky, self-esteem approaches is rubbish.

I am, however, questioning if the pendulum has swung too far in the other direction. For instance, while researching this chapter, I came across a website that read: "Taken in proper context, the attached biblical references clearly indicate that there is *no* biblical basis for self-esteem, self-love, self-acceptance, self-confidence, self-forgiveness, self-assertion, 'proper' self-image, self-actualization, or any of the other self-isms advocated by the worldly system of psychology. The Bible's answer for our emotional 'problems': turn *from* self *to* Christ (and His *all-sufficient* Word)."[11] The site went on to list 48 Old Testament and 38 New Testament passages as proof texts. I understand the need to carefully handle "the worldly system of psychology," but must all psychological insight regarding the "self" be wrong? This might make the hairs on the back of your neck stand up, but I believe there's a place for talking about confidence and esteem in youth ministry. In fact, pragmatic evidence overwhelmingly supports the need for building confidence in kids. "Studies now seem to confirm the idea that children who have positive self-esteem thrive and achieve, while those with negative feelings toward themselves are insecure, fearful, anxious, and underachieving."[12] But I believe we can even go a step further. Forget pragmatism for a moment, I believe confidence and esteem are biblical concepts!

totally empty vs. completely full

The Bible is full of verses that talk about humanity's broken, wretched, and totally ruined condition. Take a look at Romans 3:10-18:

> *As the Scriptures say, "No one is good—not even one. No one has real understanding; no one is seeking God. All have turned away from God; all have gone wrong. No one does good, not even one. Their talk is foul, like the stench from an open grave. Their speech is filled with lies. The poison of a deadly snake drips from their lips. Their mouths are full of cursing and bitterness. They are quick to commit murder. Wherever they go, destruction and misery follow them. They do not know what true peace is. They have no fear of God to restrain them."*[13]

Need more proof? Read Genesis 6, Exodus 32, Psalm 10, Romans 1, or 2 Timothy 3.

Yet, the primary message of Scripture is not that humanity's glass is empty. The central message of Scripture is that God's glass is abundantly full! The amazing truth is "God showed his great love for us by sending Christ to die for us while we were still sinners" (Romans 5:8). Do you see the progression in this verse? First is God's love, next is Christ, and finally, our sin. In other words, the cross of Christ is more about God's love and grace than about our worthiness or unworthiness. Our condition is part of the story, but it's not the central theme. The central theme is Christ! Because of Christ, and Christ alone, we can be in a relationship with God the Father. The good news might be *for* us, but it's *all about* Christ!

notice the lack of *self* in confidence

Perhaps the problem is not with the idea of confidence or esteem, but in whom that confidence and esteem are based. Should they be based in *self* or in someone else? Even more, what makes humans valuable? The message of Scripture can be tricky here. For instance, the Bible teaches humanity was created in God's image (Genesis 1:26-27), which indicates value and worth. However, it also teaches that we are absolutely and utterly ruined because of the Fall. Completely corrupt. Totally bankrupt. Worms. Pond scum. So which is it? Are we valuable or wretched?

Some claim Christ's death on the cross is proof of our worthiness. The argument goes, "Christ died for us because we are valuable. He wouldn't have died in our place unless we were worth dying for." Yet, reread Romans 5:8 and the other passages listed above. Nothing in these passages leads me to believe that I am worth dying for. "The amazing truth is that Christ died for utterly unworthy people. To minimize our unworthiness by emphasizing our value is to minimize the redemptive work of Christ on our behalf. The fact that Christ died for us is never given in Scripture as a proof of our value as wonderful people, but a demonstration of his unfathomable love. So unfathomable that he would die for *rotten* people, *wretches* like you and me."[14]

> The astronomical price of our redemption—the shed blood of God—is a testimony not of how good we are, but of how bad we really are! If we hadn't been so bad, a lower price would have been sufficient. The higher the price, the greater the testimony to our depravity, and the wondrous love of God.
>
> Randy Alcorn
> founder and director of Eternal Prospective Ministries

Have you ever considered Christ's death in this light? That his death speaks more about his attributes than our worth? I hate to admit it, but I usually view Christ's sacrifice from more of a human vantage point than a heavenly one. Perhaps it's because our culture is so selfish and inwardly focused. Whatever the reason, when it comes to personal confidence and esteem, I'm being stretched. As a child, my confidence and esteem were nonexistent. Zilch. Nada. Nothing. Enter Jim Vaught and Dan Glaze. Because of their input, my esteem and confidence grew throughout middle school, high school, college, and beyond. Much of it was tied to Christ, but looking back, much of it wasn't. Interestingly, the more success I experienced, the more my confidence and esteem grew within me verses from my relationship with Christ. By the time I reached my early 30s, I was a prideful man. I was so confident in my own abilities that I made major life decisions without significant prayer. This approach caught up with me during a youth ministry move. I walked into an ideal church and was unable to deliver the goods. It was another watershed experience; one in which God revealed the depth of my pride. I walked away humbler than I had been in years, but once again, lacking confidence and esteem.

> We are all infected and impure with sin. When we proudly display our righteous deeds, we find they are but filthy rags.
>
> Isaiah 64:6

In the years since this last watershed moment, I've come to realize that all my confidence and esteem must be based in what Christ brings to the table, not in anything I serve up. According to Isaiah 64:6, even my best, most righteous accomplishments are like filthy rags. I'm learning afresh that the good news is *for* me but is all *about* Christ. All my worth and value is in Christ, so my confidence and esteem should be in who he is, what he has done for me, and who I am in him. In fact, that's my definition of confidence: knowing Christ, realizing what he has done for me, and boldly living out who I am in him. I call this Christ-confidence as opposed to self-confidence.

why confidence is so important

Now that an explanation and definition of confidence has been established, the issue of the art of confidence having been lost in youth ministry still remains. As stated earlier, it appears that in the attempt to be more real and authentic, many youth workers have forgotten how to be confident in Christ or how to inspire Christ-confidence in students. For example, at most conferences and workshops I attend, practically all focus is given to the struggle, pain, challenge, and turmoil of following Christ. Good stuff, but not necessarily inspiring. The same can be said about the camps and retreats I attend. At least two-thirds of

> One must from time to time attempt things that are beyond one's capacity.
>
> Auguste Renoir
> 19th century impressionist painter

the themes at the retreats or conferences I speak at focus on the trials and struggles of Christianity. Again, good stuff, but have we gone too far? Is the Christian walk primarily about stumbling along, doing the best we can . . . or is there more to it? I believe there is much more to it! Yes, life is a challenge and following Christ requires sacrifice; Christ even compared it to carrying a cross (Matthew 10:38). But didn't Christ exhibit confidence throughout his challenging, cross-carrying, self-denying life? Can't we, through Christ's power, do the same? As one of my favorite sayings goes, "Life is not a journey to the grave with the intention of arriving safely in a pretty and well preserved body, but rather to skid in broadside, thoroughly used up, totally worn out, and loudly proclaiming—wow, what a ride!"[15] This is what I want! Not the assurance of

> What a new face courage puts on everything.
>
> Ralph Waldo Emerson
> 19th century American author and poet

an easy ride, but the opportunity to run hard after what really matters. Confidence, then, is important, especially when it comes to making disciples of Jesus Christ among teenagers, because it inspires us to jump on life and take the ride.

When my confidence and esteem are based in Christ, I can be who God has created me to be and do what he calls me to do. In fact, Christ-confidence inspires me in two specific ways.

Christ-confidence inspires grand dreams

When I was first in ministry, I dreamt huge dreams. Many, probably even most, were more selfish than I might care to admit, but at least they were big. Today, as a guy knocking on the door of 40, I've gotten over most of my selfish dreams. But I have to ask, "Do I still dream big?" Even more importantly, do I inspire teenagers to dream big? Do I believe God's plans are beyond what I can think or imagine? I'm talking revolutionary, transformational kind of stuff. Or . . . has the routine of life taken the revolution out of me?

How about you? Is all your talk about serving a big God just . . . talk? Do you really believe it? Do you live it?

When our confidence is in who God is, what he has done for us, and who we are in Christ,

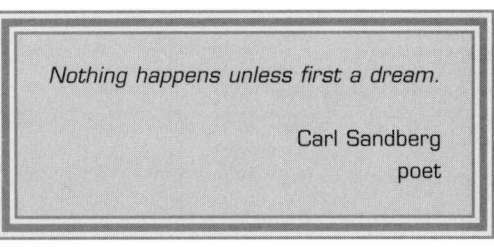

Nothing happens unless first a dream.

Carl Sandberg
poet

we can't help but dream big. Why? Because our faith and hope isn't based in our puny selves, it's based in our gigantic God. We confidently expect him to fulfill his promises. We're not sure how or when he'll make good on these promises, but we know beyond any doubt that he will. So we dream! We ask God to show us his desire for our lives and the lives of the students we are discipling. We ask him to give us his dreams about what he wants to do in and through us.

Christ-confidence inspires grand living

But we can't stop with dreaming. Dreaming is about what could be, while reality is about what is. Although we know with absolute certainty that God is always on time and on purpose, that knowledge must be fleshed out in how we live. This is why basing our confidence and esteem in Christ is so essential. It's the secret to staying energized and engaged in the disciple-making process every day—regardless of circumstances or situations. Cross-carrying and denying ourselves is hard; so hard, in fact, that only confidence in Christ can help us live above the fray and keep us in step with the Father.

This is where my concern about the trend I see in many youth workers comes into play. Their words and lessons don't inspire grand living. Optimism, joy, and excellence are replaced with pessimism, negativity, and mediocrity. It's as if sarcasm and cynicism are badges of honor. I'm all for being authentic, but let's not wallow in our depravity. Lowest common denominators don't inspire students to pursue Christ. Our pri-

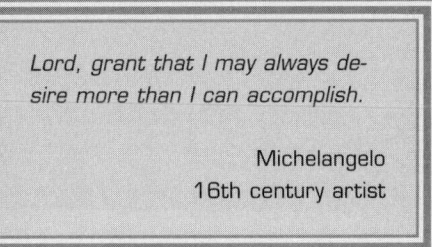

Lord, grant that I may always desire more than I can accomplish.

Michelangelo
16th century artist

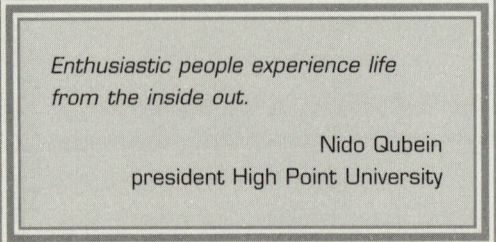

Enthusiastic people experience life from the inside out.

Nido Qubein
president High Point University

mary focus shouldn't be on where we've been, but on where we are going. As Jim Vaught taught me, let's live life with our backs to the past. There's a place for learning from failure and mistakes, so let's learn the lessons. But then, let's move on! Biblical words like faith, hope, and love aren't about being broken or shameful; they're active, future-oriented, transformational words. They're *can be* words, not *has been* words. They inspire!

Perhaps this kind of writing irritates you. Maybe you even think it doesn't have anything to do with making disciples of Jesus Christ among teenagers. "Honestly Kent, your words sound nice, but they're a bit too enthusiastic." Did you know *enthusism* comes from the Greek word *entheos*, which means "to be filled with God?" Life throws a lot of different things our way, most of which are out of our control. There is one thing, however, we can choose to control—our attitude. Why shouldn't we choose to do everything, even the hard, cross-carrying stuff, with enthusiasm? As Chuck Swindoll says:

> *The longer I live, the more I realize the impact of attitude on life. Attitude, to me, is more important than facts. It is more important than the past, than education, than money, than circumstances, than failures, than successes, than what other people think or say or do. It is more important than appearance, giftedness, or skill. It will make or break a company, a church, or a home. The remarkable thing is that we have a choice every day regarding the attitude we will embrace for that day. We cannot change our past. Nor can we change the fact that people will act in a certain way. We also cannot change the inevitable. The only thing that we can do is play on the one string we have, and that is our attitude. I am convinced that life is 10 percent what happens to me and 90 percent how I react to it. And so it is with you—we are in charge of our attitudes.*[16]

growing in confidence

As with all the of the other "art of being" elements in this book, growing in confidence is more about what God does inside us than about following a specific three-step plan. Yet, there is one specific, strategic thing we can do to create space for God to grow our confidence. As Charles Swindoll said, we can "play on the one string we have." We can take charge of our attitude. Specifically, we can enthusiastically grow in confidence by proactively doing two things.

> *In the long run, we hit only what we aim at; aim high.*
>
> Henry David Thoreau
> 19th century America author, poet, philosopher

believing in what God can do *in* and *through* you

First, every day we can choose to believe in what God wants to do in and through us. In other words, every day we either buy into what we think of ourselves, what others think of us, or what God thinks of us. Buying into what we think of ourselves is risky. When I do this, my confidence is high when things are going great, but low when things aren't so grand. What's worse, when things get bad, there is an enemy whispering in my ear, "You're a loser . . . you'll never succeed . . . how can you lead others when you trip up over the simplest things." This isn't just a case of poor self-image, it's Satan. As John 8:44 says, Satan "was a murderer from the beginning and has always hated the truth. There is no truth in him. When he lies, it is consistent with his character; for he is a liar and the father of lies." The New International Version says it this way: "When he lies, he speaks his native language." Choosing to place confidence in what I think about myself—especially when I realize Satan is constantly trying to speak his native language in my ear—is risky business.

But placing confidence

> *When you're 18, you worry about what everyone is thinking of you; when you're 40, you don't give a darn what anybody thinks of you; when you're 60, you realize nobody's been thinking about you at all!*
>
> Dr. Daniel Amen's 18/40/60 Rule
> from *The Success Principles* by Jack Canfield

and esteem in the hands of others is no better. A person's opinion of me is so fickle, especially when it comes to the roles I play in youth ministry. When I'm doing something parents like, kids might loathe me. When kids are on my side, parents might be at their wit's end. If my volunteer staff is excited about something, the church board is likely about to drop the hammer. I simply can't please all the people all the time.

The only path that makes sense is actively choosing to believe in what God can do in and through us. If you follow this course, I guarantee your confidence and esteem will soar. Guarantee is a pretty strong word. Can I really make such a pledge? Perhaps I can't, but Scripture does.

- "For you have been my hope, O Sovereign Lord, my confidence since my youth" (Psalm 71:5 NIV).
- "For the Lord will be your confidence and will keep your foot from being snared" (Proverbs 3:26 NIV).
- "But blessed are those who trust in the Lord and have made the Lord their hope and confidence" (Jeremiah 17:7).
- "We are confident of this because of our great trust in God through Christ. It is not that we think we can do anything of lasting value by ourselves. Our only power and success come from God" (2 Corinthians 3:4-5).
- "God himself has prepared us for this, and as a guarantee he has given us his Holy Spirit. So we are always confident . . ." (2 Corinthians 5:5-6a).
- "Being confident of this, that he who began a good work in you will carry it on to completion until the day of Christ Jesus" (Philippians 1:6 NIV).
- "What is faith? It is the confident assurance that what we hope for is going to happen. It is the evidence of things we cannot yet see" (Hebrews 11:1).

Wow! The Bible says the Lord will "keep your foot from being snared." It tells us our "power and success come from God." We, like Paul, have been "prepared" by God for service and given the "guarantee" of his Holy Spirit so that we can "always be confident." What's more, we can be "confident" that God will complete the "good work" he is doing in us. So, faith in God is "the confident assurance that what we hope for is going to happen."

Is your confidence soaring yet?

When it comes to the art of confidence, true assurance comes from Christ alone. Placing our esteem in our own hands or in the hands of others will sooner or later lead to our confidence being dashed. Authentic, lasting confidence comes from knowing who God is, what he has done for us, and who we are in Christ.

But . . .

We do have a role to play. Our role is to actively believe that God wants to work in and through us, especially in the area of making disciples of Jesus Christ among teenagers. The key word here is *actively*. It means we live with eyes wide-open, looking for where and how God is working. We choose to let go of cynicism and to live enthusiastically (remember, enthusiasm means to be filled with God). All circumstances, even the difficult, cross-carrying ones, are opportunities. All setbacks are potential breakthroughs. This isn't just positive, mumbo-jumbo, feel-good self talk. It's how we actively choose to "know that God causes everything to work together for the good of those who love God and are called according to his purpose for them" (Romans 8:28). It's actively choosing to trust God. It's all about our attitude!

> Though no one can go back and make a brand new start, anyone can start from now and make a brand new ending.
>
> Carl Bard
> American author

helping teenagers see what God can do *in* and *through* them

No matter what you've heard or read, today's teenagers aren't dark, pessimistic, low achievers. In fact, a clearer picture of the new generation of teens, known as Millennials, has been developing during the past several years . . .

- "There is a new generation upon us . . . they are fundamentally different in outlook and ambition from any group of kids in the past 50 to 60 years."[17]

- "The first tough, cranky, pragmatic, independent Generation Xers are gonna start hitting 40 in the next couple of years, and rearing up behind them are the Millennials... These kids are, as a group, pleasant, cheerful, helpful, ambitious, and community-oriented."[18]
- "Millennials' attitudes and behaviors represent a sharp break from Generation X and are running exactly counter to trends launched by the Boomers. Across the board, Millennial kids are challenging a long list of common assumptions about what 'postmodern' youth people are supposed to become."[19]
- "Millennials are less vulgar, less sexually active, and less violent than the youth culture adults have created for them; they are the only teen generation in recent memory for whom this is so."[20]

These aren't just nice words; they're supported by statistics and studies. Here are some results from current research:

- As a whole, teens have started backing away from early and unprotected sex.
- Teenage abortion has plummeted.
- Teen drinking, smoking, and drug use are all down.
- Teen violent crimes and suicide rates are lower.
- Today's teens are rebelling against rebellion. There's a new emphasis on manors, volunteerism, old fashioned courtesies, respect for authority, and following rules.
- Upbeat optimism and confidence are on the rise.[21]

So, let me make a prediction. Soon the tides of culture will change. Adults will see teenagers as achievers instead of slackers. They'll believe in the youth of America again. But none of these comments are my prediction. Here's what I predict: *when the American Church realizes teens are behaving better, she will assume that these kids are more spiritual than past generations.* If this prediction comes true, the Church will be making a huge mistake. Good, civic behavior doesn't necessarily constitute deeper spirituality. Don't get the wrong idea, better behavior is a very good thing, but the Church must be careful not to make the jump of assuming it means something more.

By the way, the evidence is already coming in that while teenagers today are generally better behaved than past generations, they are not necessarily more spiritual. Although "religion is a significant presence in the lives of many U.S. teens today, adolescent religious and spiritual understanding and concern seem to be generally very weak."[22] In fact, for most teenagers, religion is something "that seem quite unfocused, implicit, in the background, just part of the furniture."[23] Kids see God as a divine butler who helps them achieve success. They have bits and pieces of truth, but their understanding of the real Jesus is foggy at best.

If the American Church, then, follows my prediction and equates good behavior with being more spiritual, the fog will only thicken. Churches will be fooled into thinking teenagers are more spiritually adept than they really are and won't see the need to help them know the real Jesus better. Instead of understanding who God is, what he has done for them, and who they are in Christ, students will continue to buy into the divine butler paradigm. Their confidence and esteem, which is currently high, will likely be rocked as they grow older and realize Christ isn't a divine butler.

Perhaps the greatest calling we currently have as youth workers who are committed to making disciples among teenagers is to help this Millennial generation develop a biblical worldview so they can replace their self-confidence with Christ-confidence. By helping them pursue the real Jesus, their confidence and esteem will rest upon a solid foundation, and they will live a more God-centered life. So don't be fooled; good behavior, while good, is not best. Helping teens follow the real Jesus is what will build confidence and esteem that lasts.

true confidence!

True confidence. It's not based in accomplishments, success, personality, position, or self. Confidence and esteem that last are based in who God is, what he has done for us, and who we are in Christ. Basing it on anything else creates a shaky foundation because, while the good news is *for* us, it's all *about* Christ!

inside out questions

1. Do you have any heroes from your youth? Who are they? Why were they your heroes?

2. How would you define confidence? Who or what makes a person truly confident?

3. Why do you think confidence isn't talked about much in youth ministry today?

4. Are there dangers in being too confident? What are they? How can you keep yourself from becoming overly confident?

5. Do you dream grand dreams about youth ministry? What are they?

6. If you could see God do one thing in and through you during the next six months in regards to making disciples of Jesus Christ among teenagers, what would it be?

7. If the students in your ministry could experience God doing something extraordinary in and through them during the next six months, what would you want it to be?

8. Is there anything you can do to enhance the "confidence in Christ" environment in your youth ministry?

the art of INTENTIONALITY

by Kent Julian

The greatest tragedy of the average man is that he goes to his grave with his music still in him.

Henry Wadsworth Longfellow

*G*oals.

Virtually no word stirs up so much controversy in youth ministry.

Perhaps you didn't realize goals were so contentious. They don't get the front page attention other youth ministry controversies receive:

- Modernism vs. postmodernism
- Sunday School vs. small groups
- Camp vs. mission trips
- Student-led vs. adult-driven
- Starbucks vs. Caribou

Nevertheless, when I ask youth leaders for an opinion on goals, the responses I get are, to say the least, diverse . . .

- Goal setting is essential!
- Goals kill authenticity.

- Ministry is about investing in people, not manufacturing predetermined outcomes.
- I have goals; I just don't write them down.
- Church boards use goals to establish unrealistic, unattainable standards.
- Spiritual growth shouldn't be measured by something as worldly as goals.

No matter where you land on the goals pendulum, I want to challenge you to see goals as not only essential but spiritual. In fact, setting goals has been one of the most important, if not *the* most important, spiritual disciplines I practice!

got goals?

Before weirding out over the spirituality or non-spirituality of goals, let's first deal with the word itself. If you have a problem using the term "goals," excommunicate it from your vocabulary. Seriously, a simple change in language usually solves the dilemma for most anti-goal people. Want proof? Next time you're with someone who is vehemently opposed to goals, ask his or her opinion about intentionality. For instance, which is better . . . ?

- To be intentional in raising children or to just let things happen?
- To carefully select investments or to shake a Magic 8 Ball to determine where to put your retirement savings?
- To intentionally pick classes or randomly flip open a college handbook and enroll in the first three classes listed on the page?

These, of course, are ridiculous examples. Everyone agrees that being intentional in raising children, investing money, and attending college is essential for success. Similarly, I have yet to meet a youth worker who thinks intentionally building relationships, training volunteers, or selecting teaching topics is a waste. In fact, the opposite is true. If I suggested,

"Hey, no worries, just let things happen. Don't go out of your way to invest in students. When it comes to training volunteers, the best way to determine what to do is to shake a Magic 8 Ball. Oh yeah, and for tonight's lesson, just flip the Bible open and teach on the first verse you see." Pretty ridiculous, huh?

> Twenty years from now you will be more disappointed by the things that you didn't do than by the ones you did do. So throw off your bowlines. Sail away from the safe harbor. Catch the trade winds in your sails. Explore. Dream. Discover.
>
> Mark Twain
> 19th century American author

So if you get hung up on using the word "goals," remind yourself that intentionality and goals are woven from the same fabric. The act of goal setting is simply a proactive, deliberate approach to being intentional. In fact, goals are what move people from just talking about intentionality to creating an intended plan. If using the word leaves a bad taste in your mouth, don't dump goals themselves; simply replace the word with a more politically-correct youth ministry phrase like "intentional plans" or "strategic purposes."

yeah . . . but

You might be thinking, "Yeah, I hear you, but I'm still not convinced."

Perhaps a story will help . . .

For years, motivational speakers have championed an astonishing study that tells why people succeed. In 1953, researchers surveyed Yale's graduating seniors to determine how many had specific, well-defined, written goals. According to the study, only 3% did. Twenty years later, researchers conducted another study with the Class of 1953 and found that the 3% with goals had accomplished more financially and professionally than the other 97% combined!

Amazing story!

There's only one problem . . .

It's bogus. It never happened.

When researching material for this chapter, I read several articles

> **inside info**
>
> Wondering why goal setting is in *The Art of Being* section? Simple...like the spiritual disciplines of journaling or studying the Bible, even though it is an action, it's one that shapes a person's being and determines how a person lives.

poking fun at the motivational speakers who promote goals by using this fictitious study. Interestingly, most didn't attack speakers for their failure to check the story's validity, which would be a fair criticism. Instead they ridiculed the promotion of goals. One individual even used the following tag line to end his article, "A writer based in Kansas City, didn't graduate from Yale and never set any goals for the future."[24] It's as if he is saying, "Yeah, I hear you, but this story proves setting goals is a waste, so I'll never do it."

Sorry, but that's not what the story proves. All it proves is how important it is to check your sources. That's it! It says nothing about the validity of goals.

Obviously, the goal of this chapter (pun intended) is to convince you that having goals is essential to the ArtWork of making disciples. However, if, after reading this chapter, you decide not to set goals, be bold enough to avoid the following "yeah . . . but" explanations.

- "Yeah . . . but the study was fake."
- "Yeah . . . but I tried goals once, and they didn't work."
- "Yeah . . . but I don't see any biblical support for goals."

Most "yeah . . . but" statements are excuses—attempts to justify unacceptable behavior. Deep down, we know intentionality is important, and whether it comes about through writing goals, listing priorities, or journaling aspirations isn't the issue. The issue is that somehow, someway, we must become clear about what we believe God wants us to be and do. The reason I'm so high on goals is that whenever they are given an honest try, they work. I can't back this claim with stats or studies, yet every serious goal setter I've rubbed shoulders with has testified to the power of goals. None claim to have achieved all their goals or claim that they always set the right goals. In fact, most say they have had to learn how to adjust their goals along the way. However, those who write out goals and follow a well-thought-out action plan unanimously agree that goals are a catalyst for intentionality.

reasons to get goals

Perhaps my intentionality pep talk hasn't convinced you that you need goals. If not, here are five reasons why I believe every youth worker should get goals.

Goals help youth workers decide what matters most. Nothing creates direction like goals. They cause leaders to zero in on what matters most—which in our case is making disciples of Jesus Christ among teenagers. Think about it . . . without goals, the issue isn't whether one sees the target or not. Without goals, there are no targets! How can anyone hit, let alone aim at, something that doesn't exist? Goals create targets. They cause leaders to decide what is most important.

> Look straight ahead, and fix your eyes on what lies before you. Mark out a straight path for your feet; then stick to the path and stay safe. Don't get sidetracked; keep your feet from following evil.
>
> Proverbs 4:25-27

Goals create energy and motivation. Most people wait for motivation before taking action. "I'll get in shape, when I'm motivated." "I don't feel like preparing the lesson right now, I'll wait until I have more energy." These equations are backwards! Energy is a result of action not vice-versa. Setting goals is the forward, proactive movement of deciding what to be and do before motivation exists. Once goals are established, energy builds.

Goals make youth workers smarter. Surprised? It's true! I'm not talking about book smarts

> Opportunity dances with those who are already on the dance floor.
>
> H. Jackson Brown, Jr.
> New York Times best-selling author

(although having continuing education goals will help); I'm talking about work smarts. Youth workers with goals are clear about what's important and strategize ways to invest their time in those areas. They not only work hard, they work smart.

Goals combat temptation. Five years ago, I started traveling a lot. With a new schedule came new temptations, ones that had never particularly enticed me before. In fact, the intensity of these temptations caught me off guard. I was under the impression that, since they hadn't been an issue for 35 years, I would likely never be lured by them. Wow, was I wrong!

At first, I was able to muster up enough willpower to resist. However, as time wore on, the in-your-face nature of these temptations weakened my resolve. When I would fall, I'd quickly confess and repent; yet the next time I was on the road, I found myself in the same dilemma. It was around this time that I realized I had not been as intentional about goal setting as in the past. I had allowed the transition from one job to another to loosen my grip on goals. Interestingly, as goals became a front-burning issue for me again, the lure of these new temptations dissipated. It wasn't because I had written specific goals about resisting temptation; I hadn't. I believe it had more to do with becoming intentional once again. I was refocusing, every morning and every evening, on what mattered most. The more connected I became to my purpose and aspirations, the less appealing temptation became. This recent victory convinces me that setting and reviewing goals is one of the greatest weapons for combating temptation, and one of the reasons I consider goal setting to be a spiritual discipline.

Goals are Christ-like. I know . . . whenever Christian authors want to make a point, they thrown in the phrase "God's will" or "Christ-like" for good measure; sort of like a car salesman throwing in a year's worth of oil changes to close the deal. I resisted using "Christ-like" here, but it had to be used because it's the most compelling reason for setting goals.

Before accusing me of being a modernistic pragmatist defending the Boomer idea of goals with the name of Jesus, hear me out. Has a more intentional person than Christ ever walked the face of this earth? Mull it over . . .

- During his public ministry, did he just wake up each morning, walk around, and do random spiritual stuff?
- Or was Christ always about the Father's business—always on purpose and always on time?

Again, think deeply . . . Christ not only provided the *means* of salvation through his life, death, and resurrection, he also established a *movement* that carried the message of salvation to the world. In just three and a half years, Christ gathered a following, changed their ingrained paradigms, picked and developed key leaders, and prepared them for a future without his physical presence. I'm not saying Jesus wrote goals on a parchment Palm Pilot; but let's face it, he was extremely intentional. He had to be—the redemption of humanity rested on his shoulders!

Perhaps this is the reason he stayed in constant contact with his Father. He prayed at the beginning of his ministry (Matthew 4:1-11), during busy and demanding days (Mark 1:35-39), when his popularity soared (John 6:14-15), before picking the twelve apostles (Luke 6:12-16), just before asking his disciples if they knew who he was (Luke 9:18-21), in preparing his followers for a future without his physical presents (John 17), in Gethsemane (Matthew 26:36-44), and on the cross (Matthew 27:46). Prayer was Jesus' way of connecting with his Father, and while much of that time must have been given to relationship, don't you think some was given to discussing redemptive work? Have you ever thought of Jesus' prayers this way? If Jesus could say to his Father, "I have brought you glory on earth by completing the work you gave me to do" (John 17:4), then they had to have intentionally discussed and planned out that work.

In the same way, combining prayer and goal setting is a great way for us to be intentional about the Father's business. During times with God,

> *The best goals are not about achieving a certain standard of living, but about living a quality life.*
>
> Unknown

is there any harm in writing out what we sense God calling us to be about as a parent, spouse, disciple maker, youth worker, neighbor, and steward? Doesn't it make sense that if we write these ideas down and review them regularly, we'd likely be more intentional about what matters most? In my mind, such an approach is very Christ-like!

getting goals!

Now that you're convinced you need goals (I hope you're convinced), how do you get them? Is there an easy way to write and regularly review goals?

Yes and no.

Yes, there are simple approaches to goal setting; but no, setting and reviewing goals isn't necessarily an easy habit to develop, especially at first. However, if you do, within a short amount of time, you will receive huge returns on your investment!

> *You don't have to be great to get started, but you have to get started to be great.*
>
> Les Brown
> author of *Live Your Dreams*

What follows is a brief explanation of a three-step plan I use for setting and reviewing goals. I developed this strategy after more than 18 years of trial and error with numerous approaches. On the whole, it's a hodgepodge of ideas I've picked up from various sources and tweaked to fit me. You can and probably should modify my approach to fit your own life. In other words, don't take the ideas below as the last word on goal setting, but rather as a model that works well for me.

step one: group goals according to roles

The first step is the easiest, but most often overlooked step in the goal setting process. It starts before you ever write your first goal. It is the step of organizing, or grouping, your life around key roles.

Most people who fail to group goals together usually do so for one of two reasons. First, some people simply don't understand the importance of grouping goals. Assembling goals together under different headings is important because it helps you get your arms around your goals. Instead of having 30 arbitrary objectives, you end up with a handful of larger targets. Organizing goals this way makes the process more manageable.

The other reason people fail to group goals is because they feel like such an approach compartmentalizes life. To me, this is a valid concern. I want to live holistically, and dividing goals into categories feels like I'm being asked to divide up aspects of my personhood that can't be divided. For instance, a typical list of categories might be:

- Family Goals
- Relational Goals
- Financial Goals
- Physical Goals
- Personal Goals
- Spiritual Goals
- Professional Goals

This list creates internal conflict in me. For example, isn't all life spiritual? How can I separate spirituality from my family, finances, or career? This might seem nitpicky, but I believe it's important to set goals that are holistic, not fragmented.

There is an easy solution to this problem. Instead of grouping goals in categories, try grouping them according to the major roles in your life. Roles are different from categories—roles represent hats you wear, but they don't divide you as a person. For instance, if one of the hats you wear is that of a parent, you must bring every aspect of who you are?your physical, relational, intellectual, and spiritual being—to that role. You cannot divide out any as-

> **inside info**
>
> Setting goals concerning all the little things in life is a colossal waste of time. Set a handful of big goals around your key roles, and then break them down into smaller, daily tasks.

pect of your personhood, like spirituality, and expect to be an effective parent. Spirituality is part of who you are and must be brought to that role. So, while roles separate us by the different hats we wear, they don't divide us.

Here are the roles I have currently chosen for myself:

- *Personal Development Role*—focuses on my physical, intellectual, and spiritual development.
- *Family Role*—includes my responsibilities as a spouse, father, and son.
- *Career Role*— primarily focuses on my responsibilities as a youth leader, speaker, and author.
- *Social Role*—includes neighborhood friends, church involvement, community involvement, etc.
- *Stewardship Role*—focuses on how I handle finances, home maintenance, etc.

Here are several practical suggestions to keep in mind when deciding what roles to establish for yourself. One, keep the number of roles to a maximum of eight; otherwise, you will be overwhelmed. Two, don't try to cover every aspect of life with your roles; as long as they cover your primary areas, you'll be fine. Three, be sure to think holistically when setting goals. For example, every year I set physical, relational, intellectual, and spiritual goals as a father. Teaching my kids to ride their bikes could be a physical goal, taking each one out for a daddy date once a month could be a relational goal, establishing a plan to read classic literature at bedtime could be an intellectual goal, and teaching them the Westminster Catechism could be a spiritual goal. The key is to integrate your whole person, as much as possible, within the framework of each role.

> A dream is just a dream. A goal is a dream with a plan and a deadline.
>
> Harvey Mackay
> New York Times best-selling author

step two: write out S.M.A.R.T. goals

The second step is the hardest and takes the most time, which is probably why so few people have goals. It's the process of writing out one-year, three-year, and five-year goals. I do this annually in late November or early December, and it usually takes me 10-15 hours to complete. Although that sounds like an enormous investment of time, it pays strong dividends in two areas. First, as I've already mentioned, goals foster intentionality. I pray deeply about the goals I set and ask God to direct me to be about his purposes. The process is so spiritually significant that I devote two or three weeks of my devotional time to set goals. Second, it also pays time dividends. Having goals frees up five to ten hours a week for me. I have no way to prove this statement, but I believe it's valid. What's more, I know I invest time in what matters most, like being intentional about making disciples of Jesus Christ among teenagers, rather than wasting time on whatever feels most pressing. How do I know? I track, on a weekly basis, how I spend my time and can quickly see whether what I'm doing lines up with what matters most.

When writing goals, I use the acrostic S.M.A.R.T. as a guideline. The key word here is *guideline*, meaning each goal does not have to include every element of the acrostic. However, the more elements built into a goal, the stronger the goal.

Specific. When writing goals, be as specific as possible. Otherwise, you'll be writing good ideas instead of goals. Here are a few examples of what I mean:

Good Ideas	Good Goals
To lose weight.	I will weigh 175 pounds on June 1, 2006.
To get to know students who attend Central High School.	I will visit Central High School every Wednesday during lunch to build deeper friendships with John, Robert, Kelsey, and their friends.
To honor volunteers more.	I will write an encouragement card and send a $5 Starbuck gift card to one volunteer each month.

Measurable. Most goals need to be quantifiable. For instance, saying you are going to build better relationships with students is more of a dream than a goal. How will you build better relationships? With whom? By when? Good goals place a measuring rod on dreams so that progress can be tracked.

Attitude. When writing goals, think positive, and be proactive. Being *positive* means zeroing in on where you want to go, not what you want to leave.

Poor Example	Good Example
I will stop eating ice cream after every dinner.	I will enjoy eating a healthy fruit dessert after every dinner, with the exception of Saturday, when I will enjoy two scoops of ice cream."

Being *proactive* means focusing on the environment you want to build instead of the circumstances you face.

Poor Example	Good Example
I will not get upset when students in my small group goof off during the lesson.	Together with my small group, I will establish a *Small Group Covenant* that we all will agree with and sign by Sunday, September 21.

Some might think this advice is cheesy, but for me, it's essential. I'd much rather be positive and proactive than negative and passive. The first two words inspire and challenge, the last two deflate.

Realistic, but reaching. Goals should be stretching, yet based in reality. For example, if you are overweight, losing 30 pounds in four weeks is a bad goal. It's stretching, yes; but it won't lead to realistic change. Setting a goal to lose 30 pounds in six months, however, is a good goal. It's definitely stretching because dropping 30 pounds is an incredible accomplishment, but it is also realistic because the commitment and timeframe built into this goal will lead to a change that will enable you to stay fit for life.

The message here? Don't be a wimp. Write goals that require significant growth. But don't be foolish either; seriously consider what growth requires.

Timetable. Most goals should include a completion date. Otherwise, goals remain wishes that never get granted.

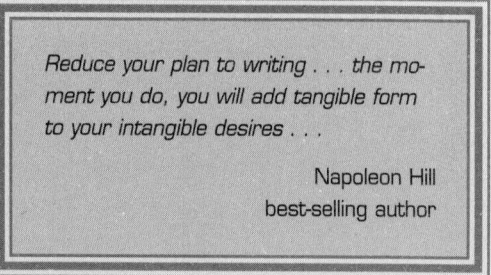

Reduce your plan to writing . . . the moment you do, you will add tangible form to your intangible desires . . .

Napoleon Hill
best-selling author

step three: develop a complete system

Even though this might sound cliché-ish, the last step is where the rubber meets the road. For years, I set goals but struggled with follow-through. The reason? Even though I had goals, I never remembered to look at them. Once I developed a system of regular review, I noticed a huge difference in my intentionality! I am much clearer, on a daily basis, about what God wants me to be and do. I'm experiencing growth in multiple areas of my life. I'm more confident, I'm getting more accomplished, and I am investing time in what matters most (like making disciples among teenagers) because I regularly review my goals.

When it comes to picking a system, there are a multitude of options from the very simple to the overly complex. The particular system you pick isn't nearly as important as just picking one. Here's the method I use. Again, it's a hodgepodge of ideas I've picked up over the years.

Yearly goals. As already stated, I write yearly goals in late November or early December. This process takes 10-15 hours. I pray about what God has for me; then I write my goals for the next year and a few three-year and five-year goals. The longer range goals are more like dreams-in-the-making concepts than specific goals.

Monthly tracking. Once my goals are established, I set aside one day a month to track my progress. In about 30 minutes, I can review my accomplishments, change or enhance my goals, and determine which goals I will work on during the next month. It's important to realize you cannot work on all your goals simultaneously. As a rule, only focus on four to six goals a month.

Weekly 20/80 list. The Pareto Principle, named after a nineteenth century economist, basically states that 20% of your activity will produce 80% of your results and success. Since I have found this to be true in virtually every area of my life, wisdom says I should emphasize the 20% as much as possible. Therefore, every week, usually on Friday, I create a 20/80 list for the next week. Doing this at the end of the week is important, because it means I already have a plan when I start work on Monday. If I wait until Monday, I fall behind before I even get started and am easily distracted by whatever seems most pressing.

> *Here are four realities that confront every youth worker I've met:*
>
> - *You'll be busy!*
> - *You have only 86,400 seconds to live each day.*
> - *You'll struggle in youth ministry if you can't manage your time.*
> - *Plan your time or people will plan it for you.*
>
> *Doug Fields*
> *from his book* Your First Two Years in Youth Ministry

Notice I do not create a task list; I create a 20/80 list. This is a HUGE distinction! I take my most important items?not necessarily the items that feel urgent, but the items that are essential to achieving my goals?and put them under the 20% column. Anything else that must be done, but isn't as vital to my goals, gets placed under the 80% column. This simple approach is my greatest tool in helping me prioritize tasks according to what matters most. It brings incredible clarity and focus.

Once I have updated my 20/80 list, I map out the next week by determining what day I plan to accomplish what tasks. I use different colored highlighters to represent different days. I highlight items in the 20% column first, then move over to the 80% column—nothing too major, just a basic "At-A-Glance" schedule.

This entire process of updating my 20/80 list and highlighting which tasks I plan to accomplish on which days takes about 20 minutes.

Daily schedule. When it comes to my daily schedule, I think about *time investment* rather than *time management*. Time management focuses on the efficient use of time; time investment focuses on the effectiveness of time. For me, effectiveness is the ultimate priority for determining how to use my time. To use time effectively, I divide my day into five blocks.

Block 1 (5 AM – 9 AM) - Devos, Exercise, and Mental Enhancement

During this block, Kathy and I spend time with God (for five or ten minutes during my devotions, I review my monthly goals and my plan for the day). Next, we get the kids ready for school, and then I go exercise. While exercising, I listen to positive, uplifting educational material (sermons, how-to CDs, etc.).

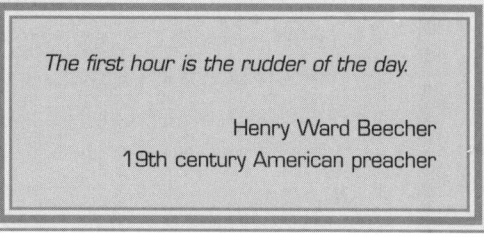

The first hour is the rudder of the day.

Henry Ward Beecher
19th century American preacher

Block 2 (9 AM – 12:30 PM) - 20% Work

I put all my effort during these hours into accomplishing items on my 20% list. At the end of this block, I usually take a 30 minute lunch break.

Block 3 (1 PM – 3:30 PM) - 80% Work

For a period of about two and a half hours, I work intensely on getting the items on my 80% list done. For me, this is usually administrative details, returning phone calls and e-mails, etc.

Block 4 (3:30 PM – 5:30 PM) - Connecting

My last few hours of work are given to proactively contacting people, whether face-to-face, through e-mail, or on the telephone. This is usually when the most relational, hands-on, disciple-making activity takes place.

Block 5 (5:30 PM – 10 PM) - Family, Read, Review, and Plan

Whenever possible, we eat dinner together as a family, play games, and read together. Once the kids are in bed, Kathy and I spend time together, read, and one or two nights a week, we watch a TV program. Most nights before I go to sleep, I spend a few minutes reflecting on the day, reviewing my monthly goals and 20/80 list, and making plans for the next day.

As you look at these blocks, please keep three things in mind. First, these blocks work for me, but your blocks will likely look different. That's fine, do what works. Second, balance your blocks. Many youth workers do a good job investing in ministry, but are lousy investors in other areas. Strive to invest well in all areas. Notice that my typical day includes investments in physical and mental fitness, family, profession, and relational connections. Such a holistic approach brings balance, variety, fulfillment, and meaning to a typical day. Third, remember all days won't be typical. The blocks above represent my *ideal* day. Some days, however, are filled with meetings. Others consist of travel. It's unrealistic to think all my days will fit into nice little blocks. The goal is to live according to these blocks as much as possible. Some days will be five block days; others will be two block days. The key is to invest time well, not necessarily to make the structure work.

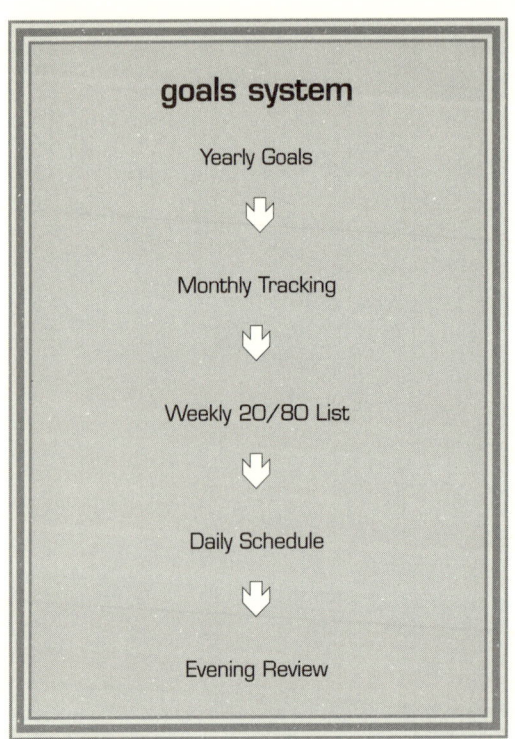

Evening review. Striving to invest your time well leads to the last, most pragmatic part of any system: establishing a daily plan that helps you implement your goals. As I have already stated, most evenings before I go to bed, I reflect on my day, review my monthly goals and weekly 20/80 list, and then create a game plan for the next day. This takes all of ten minutes. Also, I spend a few minutes during my devotions the next morning praying about my monthly goals and plan for the day. These two, simple actions are a key to staying focused. Without them, all the time I spent writing goals and creating 20/80 lists would be meaningless.

three final thoughts

All this talk about setting goals, monthly tracking, 20/80 lists, and daily schedules can feel overwhelming. Here are three final thoughts that should help you fight that overwhelming feeling and motivate you to be intentional.

K.I.S.S. it. You've probably heard this a thousand times, but the key to any plan is to *keep it simple saint* ("saint" is a bit more positive than "stupid"). For years, I tried using the newest systems and technologies to set goals. The problem? Most tools were too cumbersome for a simpleminded man like me. So even though I like gadgets, I have to keep my plan basic if I am to succeed. Here's how simple I keep things. I use Microsoft Word to write out my yearly goals, monthly goals, and 20/80 list. Then, for my daily plan, I use a 3x5 card. That's right, a 3x5 card (pretty high-tech, huh?). I write the numbers one through five down the side of the card to represent my five blocks of time, and then I list what I plan to do during each block. I like 3x5 cards because I can put them in my pocket or wallet. Plus, I use the back to record any ideas that pop into my mind throughout the day. At the end of the week, I move the good ideas from the back of my 3x5 cards to my 20/80 list. That's it, that's my plan.

> *Everyone who got to where they are had to begin where they were.*
>
> Richard Paul Evens
> author of *The Christmas Box*

Pay, then play. I've worked with enough youth workers to realize that even though many say they have goals, only about 10% actually write them down (I'm probably being generous with 10%). There are likely numerous reasons why this is true, but I believe one of the greatest is the time and effort it initially takes to set goals and establish a system. As described in this chapter, the upfront investment is high. But as Kevin Myers, the lead pastor at Crossroads Community Church in Lawrenceville, Georgia, says, "Anything of value requires a pay, then play mentality." For instance, want a good marriage? It must be paid for on the front end. Want good health? You must pay the price upfront. However, the long-term benefits of a pay, then play mentality are that you get to experience longer and better play. A solid marriage adds relational fullness to life. Eating well and exercising leads to energy and vitality. In fact, we don't pay for a good marriage or good health as much as we enjoy the benefits of them. Those who really end up paying are the ones who get the principle backwards. Those who don't invest in their marriage pay the long-term price of friction, frustration, and even separation. Those who don't exercise or eat well lose energy and vitality. So, when it comes to being intentional, setting goals is simply a way of embracing a pay, then play mentality. The upfront cost is high, but the long-term rewards are outstanding!

Start now. Finally, there is no perfect time to start, so . . . just start. Take action! Set one goal in each role and start working towards their achievement. Take little steps, everyday, and momentum will build. Think about where you could be a few months from now? Or a year from now? You'll never know unless you start. So start today!

inside out questions

1. What are your thoughts about goals?

2. Are you a goal setter? Why or why not?

3. If you write goals down, do you track your progress towards achieving goals? Why or why not?

4. Do you believe goals lead to intentionality in most areas of life? What about in the area of making disciples of Jesus Christ among teenagers?

5. Comment on the following elements of the goal setting plan spelled out in this chapter:

   - Grouping goals according to roles?
   - Writing out S.M.A.R.T. goals?
   - Developing a complete system?

6. Do you plan to use any ideas from this chapter to help you set goals? If so, which ones? Why?

7. If you already set goals, how have they helped you be more intentional about what matters most?

8. What are some other ideas regarding goals that have worked well for you?

the art of PRIORITY

by Jason Ostrander

The main thing is to keep the main thing the main thing.

Stephen Covey

During my sophomore year in college, I spent a week hiking part of the Appalachian Trail. Since I usually avoided sports that didn't involve head-to-head competition, hiking was a new adventure. If truth be told, it had always seemed a bit wimpy to me. Seriously, how difficult is it to walk?

That week, I learned a few lessons about hiking. First, walking two-by-two through rolling hills and gorgeous landscape is breathtaking. Nothing could have prepared me for the beauty. I've taken several trips back just to soak in the splendor. Second, I discovered hiking isn't for the weak! When you strap 30 pounds of hardware to your back, carry it over 15 miles of vertical climbs and descents with unsure footing, sleep on the ground, and eat half-cooked food with nothing but a pocketknife . . . let's just say the "art of walking" takes on a whole new meaning.

the art of priority = being before doing

The entire first half of this book is dedicated to the art of being. The authors believe that if youth workers are to succeed at making disciples among teenagers, they must focus on who they are in Christ before worrying about what they accomplish for him. In other words, they must learn to live from the inside out. That's why the first half of the book focuses on inner qualities like character, balance, confidence, and intentionality.

We have now arrived at the last inner quality: the art of priority. Notice, I'm using the singular form of the word "priority" rather than the plural. When I talk about the art of priority, I am not talking about lots of priorities in multiple areas, I'm talking about living by one priority—the most important priority in life. As Stephen Covey says, "The main thing is to keep the main thing the main thing."[25]

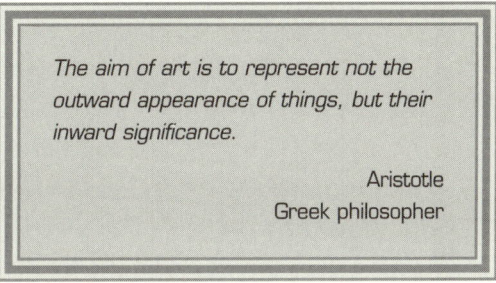

The aim of art is to represent not the outward appearance of things, but their inward significance.

Aristotle
Greek philosopher

What is the main thing? It's a growing, heart-to-heart relationship with Jesus Christ. That's it! Everything else is secondary to growing in Christ.

So if the main thing is to keep our relationship with Christ the main thing, then the art of priority is learning to actually flesh out, in real life, this being-before-doing concept. It means realizing that all the "being" qualities we've discussed in this book, as well as the ones we have not addressed, occur *because of* and *out of* your relationship with Christ. It also means that every "doing" action in the second part of this book occurs *because of* and *out of* your relationship with Christ. Basically stated, the definition of the art of priority is living a being-before-doing lifestyle. Pretty simple, huh?

This simple concept, however, is not always how I looked at life. In the past, my view was similar to my idea of hiking. Just as I associated hiking with the rather mundane task of walking, I regarded being before doing as something reserved for those who had spiritual depth but lacked an action-oriented, "let's-make-a-difference" mentality. Yet, just as my week on the Appalachian Trail taught me a lot about hiking, my ongoing journey with God continues to teach me a lot about the art of priority. For instance, I wasn't prepared for the gorgeous spiritual landscape that has opened up to me. God's splendor is breathtaking! Walking two-by-two with him, seeing his glory . . . I go back daily just to soak him up! And while the scenery of God is spectacular, the art of priority is about so much more than the view. As you know, youth ministry is anything but mundane. If you're an action-oriented person who wants to make a difference by making disciples among teenagers, you'll discover, as I have, that the art of priority prepares you for the unsure footing and the climbs and descents of youth ministry.

The Apostle Paul used a few word pictures to describe the importance of being before doing. "Now it is God who makes both us and you stand firm in Christ. He anointed us, set his seal of ownership on us, and put his Spirit in our hearts as a deposit, guaranteeing what is to come" (2 Corinthians 1:21-22 NIV). Notice how Paul puts the ownership of our very being into the hands of God. Words like "anointed" and "seal" jump off the page to show the permanency of this relationship. Even more, it is God who anoints and seals, not us. He guarantees our ability to stand firm in Christ; we can't earn it through our own efforts. We are valuable, not because of what we accomplish, but because God places value upon us. All these truths indicate that our position in Christ is the most important thing. Our accomplishments aren't unimportant; they're just secondary to our being. Again, they occur *because of* and *out of* our relationship with God. This is the gist of the art of priority.

our priority model

No other person demonstrated the art of priority better than Jesus Christ himself. Have you ever considered how much time Jesus spent preparing for ministry? The majority of his life was given to preparation, and even after he went into "full-time ministry," Jesus often slipped away to be alone with his Father. Undoubtedly, Jesus knew his first priority was his relationship with God.

Thankfully, not only did Jesus understand being before doing, he also taught it to his disciples. In the Sermon on the Mount (Matthew 5-7), Jesus introduced his followers to what true follower-ship involves, and the focus of his entire message was on inside stuff. For example, instead of preaching about the sinful act of murder alone, Jesus addressed the internal issue of anger. Also, according to the law, the physical act of adultery condemns a person; but according to Jesus, even lustful thoughts constitute adultery. Time and time again in this sermon, Jesus laid out his principles for living, all of which stem from inward conditions rather than outward actions.

pitfalls vs. benefits

If being before doing is such a simple concept, and if Jesus taught and modeled it so clearly, why do youth workers struggle with it? Why are so many caught up in their abilities or inabilities instead of God's empowerment? Why has the art of priority become a lost art? There are numerous reasons, but all of them tie into one superseding cause. Many youth workers get the order backwards and mistakenly place doing before being. Perhaps they think God's love must be earned, or they subconsciously believe accomplishments make them more worthy. Whatever the reason, the pitfalls of embracing doing over being are numerous. Here are just a few:

lack of passion

When first hired as a youth pastor for a group of about 40 high school students, I felt like the size of the group was not in proportion to the size of the congregation. To grow the group, it seemed appropriate to pull off a number of large outreach nights designed to help teenagers bring their non-churched friends to youth group. The first event centered around loud music, crazy games, and, of course, pizza. I challenged students to bring their friends and had grandiose dreams of 100-150 teenagers pouring through our gym doors. I even prepared an eloquent gospel presentation that only the hardest of hearts could reject.

So . . . you can imagine my dismay when only three new people showed up; two of which were from other youth groups in our community. After the games were played and everyone was annoyed by the deafening music, students began devouring the overestimated amounts of pizza I had ordered. I, however, couldn't eat. I was sick to my stomach. How could my students care so little about their lost friends?

Being of a hard head and full of pride, I continued hosting outreach nights for the next three months with similar results. Finally, I had a breakthrough. Up to that point, I thought a youth group was to do everything possible to grow numerically. How else could success be gauged? But, unknowingly, I was reducing ministry to the notion of doing before being. I was asking students to bring friends to meet a God they didn't really know. Do you see the irony? How could I ask students to passionately share Christ with others before giving them a chance to cultivate their own passion for him? It simply doesn't work that way. Doing doesn't produce passion, being does.

After realizing the error of my ways, I backed away from my overly zealous outreach plans and began leading students in the art of priority. Later, we re-introduced outreach nights. The outcome? A number of students introduced their friends to Christ. Since they had embraced the art of priority, they were now passionate about Christ and wanted to share his love with others.

lack of personal connection

During one of his final conversations with the disciples, Jesus reminded them of how important it is to stay connected to him:

> *I am the vine; you are the branches. Those who remain in me, and I in them, will produce much fruit. For apart from me you can do nothing. Anyone who parts from me is thrown away like a useless branch and withers. Such branches are gathered into a pile to be burned. But if you stay joined to me and my words remain in you, you may ask any request you like, and it will be granted! My true disciples produce much fruit. This brings great glory to my Father* (John 15:5-8).

Isn't John's imagery powerful? When we get the order of being and doing wrong, our personal connection with Christ is severed like a branch that is cut away from a vine. Have you ever seen a branch cut off from its trunk? The leaves turn brown and fall off. The wood becomes brittle. Termites infiltrate. In the same way, when we fail to prioritize being before doing, our personal connection with Christ is severed. Spiritually, we become brittle; the enemy infiltrates, and our lives begin to fall apart.

lack of power

The final pitfall ties into this vine analogy as well. According to John, the vine not only produces life in the branches, it also produces an abundant crop. Yet, once a branch is severed from the vine, no fruit is produced. Likewise, when we ignore the art of priority, not only is our connection with Christ severed, so is our ability to produce fruit. We lack the power to accomplish anything of spiritual significance.

creating a priority environment

Okay . . .

All this being-before-doing talk sounds pretty good, right? But it also sounds pretty lofty. Honestly, it's a pretty hard concept to get our "pragmatic arms" around, and if you're like me, you're probably wondering if anyone can actually make being "happen?"

Well . . .

Asking if a person can make being "happen" is probably the wrong question to pose. Some better questions are:

- How do we create an environment that fosters the art of priority?
- Are there certain practices we can engage that will grow our heart towards God?
- If our definition of the art of priority is connecting with God at the core of our being before attempting to do anything for him, then how can we create an atmosphere where this is most likely to happen?

Those are some good questions! In response, there are some tried-and-true suggestions that help create a being atmosphere: reading the Bible, church attendance, journaling, and prayer. Many youth workers call these "Sunday School" answers, and although these are simple answers, they are not simplistic. Each is tried-and-true for a reason—throughout Church history, these practices have helped believers create an environment that enhanced being before doing. For the purpose of this book, however, we will only focus on three environmental elements. The first one is a tried-and-true element, but it is not necessarily a discipline most youth workers have mastered. The second is a commonly used word in Christianity, but one that, in many cases, is not properly understood. The third element actually revolves around a person instead of a practice.

the power of prayer

In Mark 9:29, Jesus takes Peter, James, and John up a mountain where they witness his transfiguration. On their return down, they hear an argument breaking out in the distance and realize the other disciples are involved in a heated debate with the teachers of the law. Upon seeing Jesus, the crowd enthusiastically rushes over, and after Jesus asks what is happening, a man explains that the disciples were unable to cast out a demon from a young boy. Frustrated, Jesus casts out the demon and then withdraws. In verse 28, the disciples ask a very important question, "Why couldn't we cast out the evil spirit?" They were wondering why they were unable to do something they had done in the past. Jesus replies by saying, "This kind can only be cast out by prayer."[26]

> Until we have prayed, we can do nothing but prayer. Once we have prayed, we can do so much more than pray.
>
> Ron Campbell
> Adventures in Missions group leader

At first glance, it may seem surprising that the disciples had to be reprimanded for their lack of prayer. If they knew they were going to be involved in an exorcism, wouldn't it make sense to be prayed up? I know

I would have been! Yet, more than likely, this ministry opportunity happened like most other ministry opportunities . . . it just "popped up." Like with us in youth ministry, even though we plan dozen of exciting events, don't the most significant disciple-making opportunities usually occur in the midst of the mundane? Unplanned events that randomly pop up out of nowhere? This is probably what happened with the disciples, and since Jesus wasn't around this time, they didn't really know what to do. Additionally, I bet they had overlooked how much importance Christ put on prayer. Jesus spent hours connecting with his Father and asking for insight and power, so when he said this kind of spiritual battle can only be won through prayer, he was likely saying, "Hey guys, talent and abilities are great; but in the spiritual realm, they don't mean much. Only prayer provides the insight and power you need for difficult situations like this. That's why I pray so much."

If you are looking for a practical way to create a being-before-doing environment in your life, prayer is your first answer. It provides direct access to the Father, the kind that gives insight and power. Take, for example, my good friend Dave. After losing his wife to cancer, Dave engaged in the art of priority primarily through the practice of prayer. The more he prayed, the more God began to birth a new vision of hope within him that happened to revolve around making disciples among teenagers. Although Dave never graduated high school, he felt led to pursue a GED and then enrolled in a one-year Bible college in England.

After a year away, Dave returned. Even though he had no professional background in youth ministry, he sensed God leading him to inquire about a staff position with a parachurch organization. The position required raising support, and if you knew Dave, you'd know there isn't anything more out of line with his personality than asking for pledges. However, he got busy doing what he had to do and put every ounce of energy he had into raising support. After months of working diligently, he hit a wall. He simply couldn't crack the code to finishing off his last bit of fundraising, and even though he was ready to start, the organization would not let anyone begin without 100% support. He was at a crossroads! All his resources were exhausted. He felt like he had given every ounce of energy he could give. His God-given dream was within reach, yet he couldn't grasp it!

It was at this time that Dave went on a retreat and experienced a God moment. God revealed to Dave that, in his effort to raise support, he had taken matters into his own hands. He had accidentally reverted to doing before being. During that weekend, Dave made a conscious choice to wash his hands of the fear, doubt, and pride that had unintentionally grown within him throughout the campaign and to get back to the main thing. In his words, "God revealed to me once again his unfathomable love for me, telling me that He would be gracious with whom He wanted to be gracious." Amazingly, after returning home, the very next person Dave talked with decided to cover the remaining portion of his financial need.

Often, like Dave and the disciples, when we are unable to do something that is before us, we get caught up in focusing on our abilities or inabilities. But in reality, God does not care much about our abilities or lack thereof. His first and foremost concern is our state before Him. He wants us to know that through Him, we are capable of accomplishing anything, and he wants us to realize that spiritual battles are not won with brain or brawn, but through prayer. Dave, through prayer, won his spiritual battle. He recaptured his lost art of priority and experienced the fulfillment of the vision God had given him. Dave is now prospering as a youth worker and has been involved in making disciples of Jesus Christ among dozens, perhaps even hundreds, of students. But before he began, Dave had to learn the same lesson the disciples learned that day with Jesus—prayer is the way to connect with the one who has all the insight and power needed to overcome spiritual challenges.

the practice of faith

While prayer is a familiar spiritual practice, faith is a commonly used spiritual word, but one that most believers don't really understand. What is real faith? How is faith practiced? Interestingly, Jesus addresses this concept during the same conversation mentioned above. The identical event from Mark 9 is recorded in Matthew 17, but the highlights are from the vantage point of a different author. Instead of focusing on what

Jesus said about prayer, Matthew zeros in on Jesus' comments about faith. Jesus replied to the disciples' question about their lack of ability to cast out demons by saying, "You didn't have enough faith . . . I assure you, even if you had faith as small as a mustard seed you could say to this mountain, 'Move from here to there,' and it would move. Nothing would be impossible" (verse 20-21).

What exactly is Jesus saying about the practice of faith? There are loads of books and articles that address the topic of faith, many of which quote these very verses. Most go to great lengths to explain the multifaceted details of faith, how it works, and how to practice it. However, in my mind, the most significant truth youth workers should walk away with about the practice of faith is: *the size of our God is far more significant and important than the size of our faith*. Look back at the text. In one breath, Jesus tells his disciples that their faith is too little, but in the very next breath he says even if their faith is itty-bitty, they can still accomplish the impossible. What's Jesus saying? No matter how puny our faith might be, the size of our God is anything but puny! He is the author and finisher of our faith (Hebrews 12:2), and his ability to function, not our amount of faith, is the issue. Kent Julian often says, "If I make it as a Christian, it won't be because I'm a good follower, it will be because Jesus is a great leader. The key to success in the Christian life is putting my confidence in Jesus' ability to lead, not in my ability to follow." Think about that for a moment. At best, we are run-of-the-mill followers—at best! Jesus, however, is an exceptional leader. Therefore, the key to walking with him is found in putting our faith, no matter how large or small, in his ability to lead.

Many believers, however, get the practice of faith all wrong. They focus on the amount of faith they have instead of on the size of their God. Certain preachers even proclaim that believers must muster up more faith if they expect Jesus to do anything for them. If believers want healing, financial reward, or success, they must marshal the right amount of faith. These preachers make God sound like a giant vending machine that automatically gives out prizes once enough faith "coins" have been deposited. This is NOT a picture of biblical faith! Biblical faith is based on God being God and deciding what he will and will not do. The size of our faith, while important, isn't even in the same solar system of importance as the size of our God.

With this in mind, what does the practice of faith really look like? The Apostle Paul, when writing to a church he started, said, "We continually remember before our God and Father your work produced by faith, your labor prompted by love, and your endurance inspired by hope in our Lord Jesus Christ" (1 Thessalonians 1:3 NIV). Did you catch what he prayed for this church? He asked for a number of things, but the first was that these believers would continue to do "works produced by faith." This phrase captures the idea behind living by faith. The Christian life is not about *trying* harder, it's about *trusting* God more to work in and through us. It's about doing "works produced by faith."

Again, think about it. Does trying harder really work? If all our works, even our best efforts, are like filthy rags before an Almighty God (Isaiah 64:6), is trying really going to get us anywhere? Jim Cymbala, author of *Fresh Faith,* writes, "The most mature believer is the one who is bent over, leaning most heavily on the Lord, and admitting his total inability without Christ. The greatest Christian is not the one who has *achieved* the most, but rather the one who has *received* the most. God's grace, love, and mercy flow through him abundantly because he walks in total dependence."[27] This is what practicing faith looks like—depending on Christ for every decision, in every circumstance, in every moment! It is allowing God to be in control of every detail of life.

Perhaps the best picture I can paint to describe what the practice of faith looks like is that of driving a car. If your life is represented by a car, the practice of faith is not the act of inviting Jesus to ride in your car. You are still behind the wheel and still trying to be in control. The practice of faith is handing Jesus the keys to your car. It's turning complete control over to him and saying, "Jesus, you decide where we should go."

the person of the Holy Spirit

Finally, and most importantly, the third element to experiencing the art of priority in your life is in understanding the person and work of the Holy Spirit. As with the other environmental elements, trying to grasp who the Holy Spirit is and what He does in the lives of believers cannot be accomplished in a portion of a chapter. However, by taking a peek at the life of one of Jesus' early followers, we can better discover what the Holy Spirit can do in and through us.

With all the confusion around Christ's death and the disappointment he felt because of his denial of Jesus, Peter was quick to get back to the familiarity of his old life. Within a few days, he was out in a boat. The fishing was poor, but at least he knew how to do it. It was in this setting that Christ showed up one last time to share breakfast with Peter and help him refocus on the art of priority.

A few weeks later, in the Book of Acts, we see a different Peter—one living out such a radical faith that it's hard to believe he's the same guy. What happened? Why is he so confident? He no longer hides his association with Jesus. In fact, he can't shut up about Christ. What changed? The secret is actually found at Pentecost. In Acts 2, we read how the person of the Holy Spirit took up residence within the lives of the early believers and empowered them to live the life Christ called them to live. The fact is, without the Holy Spirit, Peter and the rest of the disciples would have likely checked out again the moment they faced any significant challenge. By themselves, they were still run-of-the-mill followers, but once the Holy Spirit came upon them, they were willing to follow Jesus—even if it meant death (and according to history, it did for most of the apostles).

Today, there are many different views concerning the role of the Holy Spirit in the lives of believers; so many, in fact, that the Holy Spirit has actually become a controversial, complicated subject. But he doesn't need to be. Jesus was very clear about the role of the Holy Spirit when he spoke to his disciples in John 14-16. Jesus stated that since he was leaving, he would send the Holy Spirit so his followers would not be orphaned without him. "And I will ask the Father, and he will give you another Counselor, who will never leave you" (John 14:16). The word *another* literally means another of the exact same kind. Jesus was promising his followers he would send another person, just like him, to give them the power needed to continue walking with him. In the simplest terms, the Holy Spirit is Christ's agent, and his job is to help believers focus on Jesus, be like Jesus, and do what Jesus calls them to do.

The power to focus. One of the Holy Spirit's roles is to make Jesus the hero of every believer's story. Even though the Holy Spirit is exactly the same in substance and ability as Christ—which means he is God and completely equal to both the Father and the Son in every aspect of his being and capacity—his role is not to champion himself. His job is to champion Jesus. This means the Holy Spirit does not seek recognition but brings recognition to Jesus. The primary way he does this is by empowering believers to focus on Jesus. As Jesus said in John 16:13-14, "When the Spirit of truth comes, he will guide you into all truth. He will not be presenting his own ideas; he will be telling you what he has heard. He will tell you about the future. He will bring me glory by revealing to you whatever he receives from me."

The power to be. In Galatians 5:22-23, we find that the fruit of the Holy Spirit is "love, joy, peace, patience, kindness, goodness, faithfulness, gentleness, and self-control." Fruit is produce. This means when the Holy Spirit lives within someone, he "produces" inward qualities. These qualities affect how we behave, but as mentioned in chapter two, they are first and foremost being characteristics. They are, so to speak, the DNA of Jesus. Therefore, another role of the Holy Spirit is to transplant Christ's DNA into the lives of his followers. As the DNA is implanted and grows, so too does a believer's ability to be like Jesus.

The power to do. Finally, the Holy Spirit also gives believers the power to do the work of Jesus, and this is especially important when it comes to making disciples among teenagers, because as we have discovered, the "commencement" command of Jesus is to make disciples. As Jesus said in John 14:15, "If you love me, obey my commandments." Interestingly, he follows this strong statement with the statement we looked at just a few moments ago, "And I will ask the Father, and he will give you another Counselor, who will never leave you" (John 14:16). In the most basic terms, Jesus is saying, "If you really love me, you will do as I ask. And since I know it is impossible for you to obey me on your own,

I will ask the Father to give you the Holy Spirit so you will be empowered to obey me."

Make the ask! If the Holy Spirit transformed Peter from a wimp to a warrior, he can do the same for us. How? Again, this is a controversial, confusing topic for many people, but it doesn't have to be. By his nature, God is a gift-giver who is willing to give unbelievable gifts to those who ask. If you want the Holy Spirit to empower you to focus on Christ, to be like Christ, and to do Christ's work of making disciples, then all you have to do is ask. Jesus said, "If you sinful people know how to give good gifts to your children, how much more will your heavenly Father give the Holy Spirit to those who ask him" (Luke 11:13). Don't make it harder than it is. "And so I tell you, keep on asking, and you will be given what you ask for. Keep on looking, and you will find. Keep on knocking, and the door will be opened. For everyone who asks, receives. Everyone who seeks, finds. And the door is opened to everyone who knocks" (Luke 11:9-10). If you want the Holy Spirit to empower you, ask! On a daily basis, ask Jesus to use his Spirit, who already lives in all believers (1 Corinthians 12:14), to help you focus on Christ, to be like Christ, and to do the work of making disciples of Christ. Just make the ask!

wrapping it up

Two final thoughts about the art of priority. First, did you notice how all the truths associated with the art of priority are fluid? The power of prayer, the practice of faith, and the person of the Holy Spirit are all intertwined. We are able to live by faith when we are empowered by the Holy Spirit, and we are empowered by the Holy Spirit when we ask Christ through prayer. All three of these are interconnected.

Second, the example of Peter should motivate us as youth workers. Peter was able to make disciples of Jesus Christ and lead the Church through turbulent years only because he had been changed at the core of his being, and God wants to do the same for us. The key is to remember that our ability to make disciples of Jesus Christ among teenagers is greatly impacted by our relationship with God. That's why the art of priority is so essential! Like Peter, we can become real warriors for God, no matter how wimpy our past might be, as long as we practice being before doing. It really is that simple.

Making disciples among teenagers has its ups and downs; but as far as I can tell, I am most effective when I live out the art of priority. Like many of my friends, however, I have been guilty far too often of putting the cart before the horse. So, as I journey further down the youth ministry road, and as we move to the next section of this book and address *The Work of Doing,* Paul's prayer for the church in Thessalonica resonates with me. May I experience "works produced by faith." In fact, if Paul were around today, perhaps he would rewrite his prayer to read something like, "I pray that you would embrace the art of priority so that you will continually grow in an ability to rely on who you are in Christ before you try to do anything for him." May it be so in my life! May it be so in your life as well!

inside out questions

1. Define the "art of priority" (i.e. being before doing) in your own words?

2. Why is the art of priority so crucial for making disciples of Jesus Christ among teenagers?

3. Have you experienced any of the following pitfalls? What have been the consequences?

    - Lack of passion for Christ
    - Lack of personal connection with Christ
    - Lack of power

4. Why is prayer so important with regards to being before doing?

5. Did you find the description of the "practice of faith" refreshing and encouraging? Why or why not?

6. How can the Holy Spirit empower you to?

    - Focus on Christ
    - Be like Christ
    - Do the work of Christ

7. What do you need to do within the next month to strengthen the "priority environment" in your life?

part two:

∙∙∙

the work of DOING

A second is equally important: "Love your neighbor as yourself."

Jesus Christ
Matthew 22:39

The man who does things makes mistakes, but he never makes the biggest mistake of all—doing nothing.

Benjamin Franklin
writer, inventor, signer of the Declaration of Independence

And in the end, it's not the years in your life that count. It's the life in your years.

Abraham Lincoln
16th President of the United States

the work of CONTEXT

by Matt Archer

He who dares to teach must never cease to learn.

John Cotton Dana

Were you a good student?

To be honest, I'm probably not qualified to ask this question. Throughout most of my educational career, I struggled to maintain a "C" average. Both my parents and teachers agreed that my poor grades were more of a reflection on my propensity to daydream than my lack of intelligence. Nevertheless, as I look back, I know exactly why I lacked focus and drive in school—I just didn't care! To be a good student, one must care about the subject matter. I didn't. Reading, writing, and arithmetic didn't do anything for me. There was, however, one subject I cared deeply about. You guessed it—P.E.!

When God knitted me together in my mother's womb, He must have been watching ESPN, because I'm wired to be a sports fanatic. I love everything about sports—watching, talking, and most of all, playing sports! So naturally, as a kid, I lived for P.E. where earning an A+ was as easy as dominating a game of four-square or thumping classmates with a dodge ball. Thanks to my passion for athletics, for one shining hour, three days a week, I was a good student.

more than passion

As I grew older, I discovered that passion alone wasn't enough to excel in sports—especially in football. To gain a competitive edge I had to become a student of the game. I read books and watched videos to learn everything I could about football. I studied pro athletes and carefully mimicking their moves. I ran stairs, lifted weights, and practiced hard. I even listened to my coaches, most of the time. By becoming a student of the game, I was able to develop as a football player.

Similarly, it takes more than passion to be effective in youth ministry. Don't misunderstand, passion is a great starting point, but youth workers who care deeply about teenagers need to spend time and energy becoming "students of the game." They need to participate in training to hone their skills. They need to learn to mimic the actions and attitudes of youth workers they respect. They even need to listen to their coaches—both the head coach (God) and his assistants (youth pastors, etc.)—to grow. Passion is crucial, but more is needed for long-term effectiveness. Youth workers who really care become students of the game!

Are you a student of the youth ministry game? If so, the second half of this book is dedicated to equipping you with some of the most fundamental skills needed to be an inside out youth worker who makes disciples of Jesus Christ among students. And perhaps the most often overlooked ministry skills is the one we are going to start off with in this chapter: *how to be a student of youth culture.*

pop quiz

Before we begin, take a few seconds to fill out the quiz below. Mark true or false next to each statement.

__ True __ False   Teenagers are proven to be better than adults at navigating Internet Web sites.

__ True __ False   In the U.S., a teenager commits suicide every 90 minutes—about 5,500 suicides a year.

___ True ___ False   A teenage girl is more likely to cause a traffic accident resulting in death than a man who's not yet 50 years old.

___ True ___ False   A higher percentage of young people graduated from high school in 1960 than do today.

___ True ___ False   Binge drinking among high school seniors is significantly higher now than in 1975.[28]

How'd you do? Did you mark all five facts true? Four? Three? Two? Only one? You might be surprised to find out that all the facts are false. Yup, every single one. If you answered true to most of them and are beginning to question whether you are qualified to work with teenagers . . . don't! The goal of this exercise was not to make you feel guilty but to show you that, in many cases, our preconceived ideas about the teenage world are incorrect. Let's take a closer look at why some of our mental models concerning youth culture are wrong and how we can go about becoming better students of youth culture.

bridging the culture gap

One of the most difficult aspects of staying relevant in youth ministry is the ability to connect and communicate with teenagers. Youth workers in their early 20s often connect and communicate easily, even naturally, simply because of their age. However, these same youth workers, by the age of 28, are ten years removed from high school, and what once seemed easy now proves much more challenging and even awkward. For example, a youth worker who, at one time, effortlessly crafted lessons that connected with teenagers now spends twice as long preparing only to be crushed when her students respond with blank stares and looks of disbelief—as if she were speaking in a foreign tongue or had suddenly sprouted a third eye. If you've ever felt like you and your students are living in two different worlds, you're probably not far from the truth.

Here's the deal . . .

Most youth workers are at least one life stage beyond their students. Take those young youth workers mentioned above, the ones who find it rather effortless to relate to teenagers. The fact is even they are at a different life stage than teenagers. They are at the "entering the professional world" stage, while their oldest youth group member is at the "entering college" stage. Even though there is only a four- or five-year age difference, there is a significant distinction in life stage. Consequently, these young youth workers, while finding it less challenging than their older counterparts to connect with teenagers, still experience some sort of communication gap whether they are cognizant of it or not. What's more, the older they become, the more life stages get inserted, and as a result, the communication gap grows larger and larger. This gap can be summed up in one word—culture.

The word "culture" comes from the Latin word *cultura*, which means to till, plant, and grow. The original idea of culture came from agricultural societies where the harvesting of crops was crucial to survival. Today, culture is used to represent much broader concepts like human growth and development and to define one's social identity. For the sake of this chapter, we will narrow these broader concepts down by identifying culture as *a specific way of life that is shared by a particular group of people.* This means youth culture is the way of life (the beliefs, perceptions, thoughts, feelings, and social reactions) shared by a specific generation of teenagers.

Just like when we grew up, today's teens process every piece of information they receive through the filter or grid of their culture. This filter is a powerful force in their lives and has the ability to shape, direct, or limit their thinking. Since you and I do not share the same cultural grid, we face considerable roadblocks in connecting and communicating with teenagers. In addition, if the outcome of all we do in youth ministry hinges on our ability to connect and communicate, these roadblocks are perhaps the most daunting challenge to effective youth ministry.

What does this mean for youth workers?

It means we must become students of culture!

If we truly care about making disciples among teenagers, we cannot expect them to bridge the cultural gap; we must step onto their turf by becoming students of their world. As we do, we will recognize some realities that are similar to the ones we faced as teenagers and others that are totally unique to them. It will be risky, exciting, even daunting. Nevertheless, if we really want to connect and communicate effectively, we must become students of youth culture—no matter what our age or background.

How do we do it? By developing and practicing three skills: prayer, observation, and engagement.

students of culture pray

Even though Jason addressed the practice of prayer in the last chapter, we're going to start off talking about it as well. Looking at prayer as a youth culture skill might seem a bit odd. Perhaps you think I'm being pseudo-spiritual or trying to validate the need for cultural relevance by throwing around the concept of prayer. Actually, the exact opposite is true. As you have probably realized, being culturally relevant is all the

---

outward action

The Prayer Rolodex

Step 1: Break out the digital camera and take mug shots of every student in your ministry willing to say "cheese."

Step 2: Place each picture on a 3x5 card to create a Youth Group Rolodex.

Step 3: Keep this Rolodex on your desk. Whenever there is a break in the action, pray for one or two students. When you reach the end of the Rolodex, turn back to the front and start over again.

Step 4: To make this practice more powerful, write students' e-mail addresses on their Rolodex cards. Each time you pray for a teen, tell him or her in an e-mail. You'll be blown away with students' appreciation, as well as the relational connections you build.

rage in youth ministry today. Books, seminars, and magazines are constantly championing the need to understand culture. But in the midst of all the noise, it's easy to forget that the most powerful and practical action we can take in any area of ministry is prayer.

As youth workers, we are disciples first and disciple makers second. As disciples, prayer should be one of our highest values because prayer is our primary method of connecting and communicating with Jesus. It is the means by which he enables us to face the inevitable challenges that await us throughout the journey of life. But in our role of disciple maker, we also need to be prayerfully dependent because prayer gives us the divine insight we need to effectively grow students into followers of Christ. In other words, prayer is not just essential to the *art of being*; when it comes to ministry, it is essential to the *work of doing*. I will even go so far as to say prayer is the first and most important work in any disciple-making endeavor. As Carl Wilson writes, "Prayer is one of the most important aspects of building disciples. If one is to help others grow in the knowledge of Jesus Christ, he must pray. Indeed, if one does everything else in terms of building disciples, yet fails to pray, nothing significant will happen."[29]

Prayerful dependence is especially important when attempting to make disciples among teenagers because of the spiritual bondage that ensnares so many kids. Teenagers are often blind to the truth of God largely because the constant messages advanced by culture have grown deep, deceptive roots in their lives. In Mark 9:14-29, Jesus taught his disciples that some spiritually enslaved people would never have the blinders of sin removed unless serious prayer was offered on their behalf. If this is true, then the most fundamental responsibility to being culturally relevant is not watching MTV or observing students at the mall; it is standing in the gap for students through prayer. This is why prayer is our first and most important work in being a student of youth culture.

students of culture observe

When a teenage guy struts into a youth meeting with his baggy pants riding low over his boxers and his Oakland Raiders cap twisted slightly to the side, what is the first thought that enters your mind? Be honest . . . remember, this is a Christian book. Or how about when a young lady shows up for worship team practice wearing barely enough t-shirt to cover the region between her shoulders and her diamond studded navel? If your initial reaction to strange hair, provocative clothing, body piercing, stand-offish attitudes, or *(place a confusing cultural expression from your list here)* feels like a schizophrenic mixture of confusion, compassion, and contempt—then congratulations . . . you're totally normal!

Expressions of contemporary youth culture are evident everywhere, and short of putting your head in the sand, they are virtually impossible to avoid. Yet admittedly, retaining objectivity is challenging. Even as a veteran youth worker (that's church lingo for "old person"), I find objectivity difficult primarily because I am locked into my own cultural grid. My initial response to new, quirky, teenage styles is to judge them

---

outward action

Want a better glimpse of youth culture? Check out popular media. Here are a few practical ideas . . .

Audio: Whether you're driving your car or the church van, let students control the radio. This simple action will give you an idea of what kids listen to. As you groove to the tunes, process the music's messages with them.

Video: Take a group of students to a movie with one catch . . . they pick the flick. Afterwards, grab a shake and some fries while talking together about the messages being promoted.

Print: Go to your local bookstore with one of your teenagers and ask her to pick out two copies of her favorite magazine. Pay for the magazines, give her a copy, keep the other for yourself, and then enjoy a cup of java together as you flip through different articles and advertisements.

Internet: The internet is the Nirvana of modern media; it brings every form of media together under one umbrella. Be sure to become familiar not just with websites and blogs you like, but check out the ones that are favorites among students.

as strange, wrong, or even evil. However, if I want to make disciples among teenagers, I have to be willing to step outside my own filter and look at cultural expressions from the perspective of teenagers. Why do they dress a certain way? Why are they saying certain things? Why the attitude?

In the summer of 1992, I traveled with several high school students on a weekend field trip to New York City. When the journey began, the atmosphere inside our 15-passenger van was electric; we could hardly contain our excitement about visiting America's largest city. Once we arrived, we stopped at plenty of famous landmarks, and although we enjoyed each sight, we also became disenchanted with the Big Apple. In our minds, it was failing to live up to its hype. Since we spent most of our travel time on the subway, we weren't gaining an appreciation for the enormity and complexity of the city that loomed above us. From our subterranean vantage point, the landscape and scenery changed little as we traveled from borough to borough. By the time we headed to our final tour stop, none of us realized that our perception of NYC had been unfairly skewed by a less than flattering perspective.

Stepping off the elevator onto the observation deck of the World Trade Center instantly changed our perspective. We were captivated! What we earlier dismissed as "just another city" was suddenly a gleaming masterpiece of metal and glass stretching beneath us in every direction and beyond the horizon. As the sun set, we watched—awestruck—as the lights came up across midtown Manhattan. In that moment, I realized what a difference perspective makes.

Youth workers must be willing to occasionally step outside their own cultural grid and look objectively at the world from the perspective of teenagers. Developing this ability isn't easy, but it can be done. Here are four important truths to keep in mind when attempting to look at the world from the perspective of teenagers . . .

youth culture is real

John Rosemond, in his book *Teen-Proofing: Fostering Responsible Decision Making in Your Teenager*, reminds parents they are not the only force in their child's life.[30] Youth workers would do well to adhere to the same advice. No matter what you think about youth culture, the reality is that it is a very real and powerful force in the lives of students. Remember our working definition of youth culture? "The way of life (the beliefs, perceptions, thoughts, feelings, and social reactions) shared by a specific generation of teenagers." Since today's generation of teenagers has its own cultural "personality," many of their beliefs, perceptions, thoughts, feelings, and social reactions are different than those shared by adults. Not better or worse, not necessarily good or evil . . . just different. Wise youth workers learn the uniqueness of today's youth culture, validate its impact, and equip teens to discern which messages are true and which are false.

subcultures are real

The existence of various subcultures makes observing and understanding youth culture even more complex. What is a subculture? When a group of teens behave differently than what is deemed "normal" by popular youth culture, a subculture forms. Home schooled teens are a good example of a subculture. They often have their own set of shared beliefs and social responses that are unique from what popular youth culture considers normal.

How a subculture is viewed and treated by the popular majority depends greatly on just how unique the subculture is. The greater the difference, the more likely the group will be shunned. For example, Goth is a subculture that has experienced significant rejection. Their fashion style and behavioral patterns are far outside the realm of normalcy for the typical, upbeat, civic-oriented Millennial teenager (for a description of Millennials, see chapter four). Once again, wise youth workers learn to recognize the distinctive characteristics of different subcultures and develop appropriate disciple-making approaches for each.

God loves every student

Remember the first Bible verse you memorized? It was probably John 3:16, which teaches that God loves each person so much he willingly made the ultimate sacrifice to save us from sin. Regardless of how teenagers view God, this verse tells us that God looks upon them with the same undying compassion he has had for humanity from the moment he breathed life into Adam's dust-filled lungs.

The apostle Paul, an ambassador of God's love message, wrote, "I try to find common ground with everyone so that I might bring them to Christ" (1 Corinthians 9:22b). Shouldn't youth workers, who are modern day ambassadors of the same message, find common ground with teenagers? Perhaps you have difficulty getting past some of the offenses of contemporary youth culture. If so, try remembering what it was like to be young and impressionable. Look back at the oddities and influences from your pasts to find common ground with teenagers. Whenever I venture down this nostalgic path, I usually arrive at the same destination . . . if God loved me with my parachute pants and my Bon Jovi buttons plastered all over on my denim jacket, then surely He loves the kid in my ministry who looks like the offspring of Alice Cooper and Elvira. Go ahead, try it yourself—journey back to your nonconformist teenage glory days (you rebel, you). Remember how, at the fresh age of sixteen, you trusted the messages espoused by your culture? Remember the disdain you felt towards "the man?" Fortunately for most of us, there was an adult or two who took time to see the world from our perspective. They acknowledged the substance and significance of our culture, even though they probably disagreed with most of its messages. They gained our attention and trust by resisting the urge to dismiss our cultural expressions. More importantly, they understood that Christ loved us and were willing to stick with us until we recognized our need for him (which, by the way, brings us to our fourth truth).

you are God's missionary

It has been clinically proven, probably by the same research group that polls dentists about sugar-free gum, that four out of every five youth workers, at one time in their lives, whispered the prayer, "Okay God, I'll do anything for you, but please don't ask me to be a missionary." So, instead of sending us across the ocean, God, in His infinite wisdom, sent us across the hall to the youth room (somewhere in heaven there is a still, small voice whispering, "Gotcha!").

The term "missionary" can be generally defined as: *one sent by a church to make disciples of Jesus Chris in another culture.* Now don't miss this! There is no other segment of ministry in the American church today that shares more similarities with global missions than youth ministry. As a youth worker, you may never have to evade cannibalistic pygmies armed with blow-guns or live in a grass hut without an X-Box, but make no mistake about it—you *are* a missionary!

There are three central missiological principles every missionary must follow to effectively make disciples among a people-group. First, they must have a passion for the people-group they are attempting to reach. Second, they must also gain a competent awareness of the native culture. Finally, missionaries must become fluent in the native dialect. When missionaries practice these missiological principles, they gain a context for ministry.

The same principles are required of us. Passion for a specific people-group, competent awareness of their unique culture, and the ability to communicate in their native dialect—these are the principles required to gain a context for youth ministry. Like missions, youth ministry takes contextualization. And like missionaries, youth workers observe the world students live in—not to become part of it, but to attain a context for making disciples within it.

students of culture engage

Understanding that youth ministry is synonymous to missionary work leads to the third skill needed for being a good student of youth culture. Comprehension of youth culture, while vital, does not mean youth workers automatically develop an ability to make disciples of Jesus Christ among teenagers. To do so, youth workers must put their new understanding to practical use by *engaging* youth culture.

Every once in a while, I have so many ideas bouncing around my brain that it's nearly impossible to get a peaceful night's rest. One night, after tossing and turning for hours, I reached for the only effective cure to insomnia I know—the remote control. Clicking through 98 channels of basic cable, I finally found one show that was sure to knock me out; it was an old movie titled, "The Boy in the Plastic Bubble." In this action-packed thriller, a young John Travolta masterfully portrays a teenage boy with a less-than-stellar immune system. To deal with his affliction, Travolta's character was forced to live inside a big plastic bubble that resembled a giant gerbil ball. For ten and a half minutes, I was absolutely riveted by the drama; then suddenly, without warning, I drifted off to slumber land.

Though I fell asleep, I did gain a decent illustration from this flick. Why do we sometimes try to build plastic bubbles to protect teenagers from the dangers of culture? Think about it . . . instead of training teens about how to live within their world, we are often tempted to figure out bulletproof ways to protect them from their world. But like the air we breathe, youth culture is everywhere, and whether we like it or not, the airborne particles of culture will impact students. That's why our job in making disciples isn't to be bubble builders, but to help students develop a *biblical worldview filter* with which to process the messages of culture.

a biblical worldview filter

A biblical worldview filter . . . I know what you're thinking—it sounds kind of churchy, right? Why would an ultra hip, off-the-hook, super cool youth guy like me recommend something so lame? Because helping students develop a biblical worldview filter might be the most culturally relevant method of discipleship available today! Let me give you an example . . .

It's Friday night, and you've agreed to meet a couple guys from your high school group, Toby and Brady, at the local movie theatre. "Which show are we watching tonight boys?" you ask. " 'Hellboy'!" Toby responds. "You invited your youth group leader to 'Hellboy'?" Brady looks up with a sheepish grin, "I guess we got issues." Everyone laughs as you head into the theatre.

After the feature, you grab a milkshake with the guys and reminisce about the cinematic feat that was "Hellboy." Toby and Brady both agree the fight scenes rocked. "What was your favorite part?" Brady asks. "Well, I really liked when the old guy said, 'In the absence of light, darkness prevails . . . There are things that go bump in the night, we are the ones who bump back.' That line reminds me of us." After a moment of awkward silence, Toby ventures, "What do you mean?" "As Christians, Jesus says we are the light of the world. Our world is pretty dark, and if we don't reflect the light of Christ, then darkness will prevail. But when we're bold about our faith, we are the ones who bump back against the forces of evil." More silence, then Brady says, "Whoa, pretty cool!"

There you have it; you have just effectively modeled a biblical worldview filter by engaging culture and connecting it to biblical truth in a way that reflects critical thinking (by the way, that's the definition of a biblical worldview filter). The more you teach and model critical thinking, the more students will develop the ability to "talk back" to the messages of culture. Instead of a message seeping in unnoticed, it is either confirmed with a "that's true" or confronted with a "wait a minute, that's a lie." It's a skill all believers should have—especially teenagers. And you thought it was going to be lame . . .

I'm not exactly sure who first popularized the idea of a biblical worldview filter, but I'm going to credit Rick Lawrence, editor of *GROUP Magazine*, because he sure talks about it a lot. Rick recently had this to say about the purpose of engaging culture. "When Jesus used fishing, farming, money, or common cultural practices to unveil his good news (bad news to some), he was bridging God's transcendent truths into the everyday world of the people. We must do the same . . . It's time to reassert our identity as people who live in the world but are not of it. It's time to focus on training young people to think critically about their cultural influences."[31] Preach it Rick!

in the world, but not *of* the world

Before getting too excited about using movie clips or song snippets to bolster youth talks, check your motives. Engaging youth culture for the sake of being edgy or cool isn't the point. Youth culture should only be engaged to help students develop the skill of being in the world without becoming part of it. Youth culture is a dangerous mistress because its negative messages are so alluring, so you must have a keen awareness of the dangers.

> Don't become so well-adjusted to your culture that you fit into it without even thinking. Instead, fix your attention on God. You'll be changed from the inside out.
>
> Romans 12:2a
> The Message

For the most part, the negative messages propagated in youth culture haven't changed in 40 years; they still focus on alcohol, drugs, violence, sex, and secularism. What has changed is the frequency and audacity with which they are delivered. Take the subtle messages that sex outside of marriage is inconsequential. Practically everyone admits teenagers are growing up in a world saturated by sex. But did you know that from 1999 to 2000, the increase in sexual references on television during 'family hour' was 74%?[32] Can you say "frequency and audacity?"

With all its destructive messages, engaging culture might appear to be the last thing Christians should do. However, the imminent danger is precisely *why* youth workers need to properly engage culture and train teens to do likewise. When churches fail to teach people how to intelligently interact with culture, they become irrelevant. As a result, lost people view Christians and God himself as irrelevant. Although the Bible warns Christians not to be *of* the world, it also teaches them to be *in* the world. Steve Turner described this well when he writes, "We become worldly not by engaging with the world, but by allowing it to shape our thinking. Jesus prayed to God 'not that you take them out of the world, but that you protect them from the evil one' (John 17:15)."[33] In other words, Jesus' desire for believers is to remain in the world, not to be shaped *by* it, but to have opportunities to shape those *within* it. This is why engaging youth culture is so important—it gives youth workers the opportunity to make disciples among teenagers. Plus, when students are trained to use a biblical worldview filter, they too have opportunities to make disciples among their friends!

class is now in session!

The students we serve are a reflection of their culture. Every thought they think, every word they speak, and every action they take is affected by this culture. Therefore, if we truly care about making disciples among teenagers, we'll become students of youth culture. Sure, it takes time, but it is well worth the energy and effort. Becoming students of youth culture allows us to better connect and communicate with teenagers. It will also give us an understanding of their world and the challenges they face. It will even enable us to better equip teens with the knowledge, skills, and attitudes they need to be followers of Jesus Christ within their world.

So . . . be a student of youth culture. Observe. Engage. But above all else, pray!

Okay, there's the bell. Class is now in session. What kind of student will you be?

inside out questions

1. Why isn't passion for making disciples of Jesus Christ among students enough to be effective? What else is needed?

2. Are you a student of youth culture? Why or why not?

3. Do you struggle with a cultural gap when working with teenagers? In what ways?

4. Have you ever thought of yourself as a "missionary" to students? How would doing so enhance your ability to make disciples among teenagers?

5. Do you have any concerns about helping teenagers engage youth culture? Does the concept of helping students develop a biblical worldview filter soften your concerns?

6. What are the dangers of using the biblical worldview filter approach? What are the benefits?

7. What is one thing you want to do to become a better student of youth culture?

08 the work of AFFECTION

by Guy Wasko

Do not waste your time bothering whether you "love" your neighbor, act as if you did.

C.S. Lewis

Isn't it interesting how some of the most beautiful, cherished, transforming events in our lives are tightly woven around major blunders or mishaps?

I will never forget the night my daughter was born. What a beautiful moment! Months of preparation, expectations, and fears precipitated the evening. Finally, Emma Grace was born. She was amazingly small and precious. She had amazingly strong lungs (a trait inherited from me). And she was amazingly beautiful (a trait definitely inherited from her mom). I couldn't wait to hold her. Even more, I couldn't wait to hand her to her mommy for the first time.

If you've been through the birthing experiencing, you know there are certain steps—the first bath, the weighing in, and cutting of the cord—that must transpire before the official handoff to mom can occur. For me, this is where the cherished moment thing inevitably intersected with a blundering gaffe. Forever, the two shall be joined.

As in most delivery rooms, there was a small warming table approximately ten feet away from the bed where Emma was delivered. That's where the medical staff would clean her, make sure all her little parts were functioning properly, and allow her shivering, naked body to warm up. However, before Emma could be taken to the table, one other thing had to happen. Yep, you guessed it, the umbilical cord needed cutting. As tradition would have it, it was the father's privilege. I believe the faux pas went something like this...

"Well Dad, it's time to cut the cord," the doctor said as she handed me the scissors.

With all sincerity, from the depths of my soul, I pointed toward the warming table parked across the room and said, "Okay. Here or over there?"

As you can imagine, the nurses thought this was one of the all-time funniest replies in the history of the hospital, and they certainly let me know it. To this day, my wife and I still laugh about how insightful and incredibly wise my response was that night.

love as a lifeline

Similar to how an unborn baby's sustenance comes from an umbilical cord, love is a lifeline to health and vitality in youth ministry. Not just any love—divine love. The kind of affection we can't muster up ourselves; the kind that finds its source in God.

There are many skills needed to be an inside out youth worker who makes disciples among teenagers, and knowing how to create an atmosphere of love within ministry is as fundamental as it gets. It was fundamental to Christ's ministry, as we will see. In addition, when considering the cultural challenges mentioned by Matt in the previous chapter, perhaps there is no greater skill to learn. It's more important than knowing how to organize an event or develop the world's greatest lesson because it brings sustenance, health, and vitality to a youth ministry. Again, it's a lifeline. As Jesus said, "All the other commandments and all the demands of the prophets are based on these two commandments"—love God and love others (Matthew 22:40).

The good news is, as an inside out youth worker, you have the ability to create an irresistible atmosphere of Christ-like affection in your ministry right now. How? By becoming a relational environmentalist!

the DNA of environmentalists

Relational environmentalists? Who are they? What do they look like?

The best way to describe relational environmentalists is to compare them to ecological environmentalists. Ecological environmentalists, the people commonly referred to as "environmentalists," see ecology as a

> ### outward action
>
> Here are some steps you can take to become a more affectionate, caring person:
>
> - Seek other people's input. Find someone who is at least one step ahead of you in expressing love and learn everything you can from that person.
>
> - Each month, focus on one aspect of the nine love qualities found in I Corinthians 13:4-8a. Study the aspect, pray about it, and apply it to your life.
>
> - Focus on being a loving spouse, parent, work associate, and friend. Remember, love needs to be part of your DNA, not just a "hat" you wear around students.
>
> - Answer the question, "What one step can I take in the next 90 days to drastically improve my ability to love?" Then, take that step!

cause. They rally, volunteer, sponsor, protest, fight, and invest in anything and everything that they think will improve nature and protect her from pollution or destruction. Most environmental advocates would go as far as saying the title "environmentalist" is more a characterization of who they are than a description of what they do. Protecting the ecosystem isn't something they can stop thinking about or turn off; it's a part of their DNA.

Before you think I'm about to propose a fund-raiser that involves picketing a major oil refinery, consider the implications of environmentalism. Taking care of God's natural world is important, so true ecological environmentalism is certainly a worthy cause. Yet how much more worthwhile is enhancing a teenager's world with authentic, divinely inspired affection? Isn't improving a ministry environment just as high a calling? To me, creating a loving atmosphere that is conducive to seeing life-change—to seeing God do his thing—is priceless!

How can such an environment be created and enhanced? The place to start isn't with ministry structure, programs, or outreach events. It's not even with practical ideas that you can apply during your next meeting. It's with your heart! Are you a relational environmentalist at the core of your being? Is love something you turn on and off, or is it a part of your DNA? To find out, see if you have the DNA qualities of a hardcore environmentalist.

environmentalists are advocates

True environmentalists have no problem promoting their cause. They understand what they are fighting for and intently, even aggressively, forge ahead with their agenda. Their passion fuels their "whatever it takes" attitude.

Are you an advocate of affection? Is it your agenda? How passionate are you about it? When people mention your name, can they separate who you are from what you stand for—love?

environmentalists are watchdogs

Environmentalists are students and lovers of the ecosystem. Because they know about and love the environment so much, they can quickly spot when something isn't quite right within the world. They know when there is a problem with the climate and understand the implications of pollution. Yet they don't stop at understanding. Their mission includes "barking" out warnings of potential repercussions to the rest of the world.

As relational environmentalists, how do we know when something isn't quite right within our relational world? Can we identify problems in ministry that could potentially erode the foundation of love and affection in our group? Are we bold enough to bark when we spot gossip, spitefulness, callousness, or other relational dangers?

The key, of course, is to be the right kind of watchdog. We've all seen ecological environmentalists who chain themselves to trees or lay in front of bulldozers. They're watchdogs alright, but they're like those obnoxious yappy dogs that never stop barking. After a while, no one pays attention because they've cried "wolf" too often. That's not the kind of watchdog relational environmentalists should strive to be. True relational environmentalists won't sniff out every little problem or bark at every dramatic dispute (remember, we work with teenagers . . . drama happens). True relational environmentalists strive to be a "man's best friend" kind of watchdog. They are loyal and trustworthy. They look for the best in others, and when they bark, it's only because "wolves" are actually around.

environmentalists are recruiters

Ecological environmentalists are awesome at enlisting others to join their cause. They recruit individuals, non-profit organizations, companies, and politicians because they realize a team has far greater impact than an army of one. They are so good at getting others involved that many people referred to them as activists.

Are you an affection activist? How good are you at campaigning for the cause? Do you have a team of people who share your passion for loving teenagers? You don't need to be a great salesperson to recruit others. If you love students, that love will naturally overflow out of you and be your best recruiting tool.

environmentalists are influencers

Ecological environmentalists strive to influence others about the importance of their cause. Rallies, marches, protests, personal interaction, campaigns, the political process—these are just some of the techniques they use to make their case. Environmentalism has gained momentum over the years precisely because its followers are so good at winning others over. They've convinced many people to see the world through their lenses.

How are you at influencing others to see the world through "love lenses?" Have you convinced others of the importance of loving teenagers in your group?

Early on in ministry, I learned not to underestimate what God does through, and often in spite of, me. Perhaps you, like me, have come home some nights after youth group completely discouraged because you missed a chance to connect with a kid or fumbled over a lesson so badly that not even CSI's Gil Grissom could find its central meaning.

> Nothing else can quite substitute for a few well-chosen, well-timed, sincere words of praise. They're absolutely free and worth a fortune.
>
> Sam Walton
> founder of Wal-Mart

Yet, isn't it just like God to do something incredible on those night? One night, I received a phone call after a long, grueling day. A familiar voice greeted me, and we began to catch up. The call was from Jessica, a student from a former ministry. We spoke for quite a while—just making small talk at first—and then she began asking for advice. Jessica had made some bad decisions and found herself at the end of a very long rope. In her greatest point of need, she called her former youth worker—the guy who was convinced he wasn't making much of a difference. To this day, I have no idea how Jessica got my out-of-state phone number. I do know, however, that she called me because she felt like I cared. As I hung up the phone, I vowed to never again doubt God's ability to work through imperfect followers like me. Even more importantly, I also committed anew to influencing others to see teenagers through the lenses of love.

a new rule for environmentalists

How did you line up with the DNA qualities of an environmentalist? Is relational environmentalism intertwined around the core of your being or is love something you turn on and off? No matter where you currently fall on the affection spectrum, you can grow in your affection skills by learning to live by a new rule. It's actually not a new rule; it's just a new way of looking at three ancient principles. Each principle builds on the others to bring about a complete picture of Christ-like love.

the golden rule

If asked to recite the Golden Rule, you'd likely have no problem. "Do unto others as you'd have them do unto you" is an age-old moral code that transcends most religious lines. It's even crossed over into the areas of business, leadership, and best-selling books. It has become universally accepted because of the results it produces.

But if you're like me, the Golden Rule leaves you wanting more. It doesn't feel like the ultimate standard of love. Is this all the Bible says about love, or are there other standards that challenge us to express a deeper, more powerful form of affection?

the platinum rule

Perhaps you've heard of the Platinum Rule.[34] This rule encourages one to "treat others the way they want to be treated." Catch the difference? Instead of treating a person the way you'd like to be treated (i.e. Golden Rule), you put yourself in the other person's shoes and treat him or her how he or she wants to be treated (i.e. Platinum Rule). It forces you to step outside of yourself and think more deeply about the needs of another. The Platinum Rule calls for more than the Golden Rule, because it requires more intentionality.

But again, is it the ultimate? Is there something grander? Is there something that gives a fuller, purer picture of Christ-like love?

the titanium rule

In the world of jewelry, a new metal is taking over. The new trend from wedding bands to watches is titanium, and in many ways, titanium is becoming the new gold. As we consider the truths that guide our deepest motivation for loving teenagers, perhaps it's time to trade up to a new rule—the Titanium Rule!

Before revealing the Titanium Rule, let's be sure we're on the same page. The Golden Rule is good (it's biblical, for goodness sake), but does it give a complete picture of Christ-like love, or is it just a piece of the puzzle? I would argue that it reveals part of Christ's love picture, but not all of it. In the Golden Rule, "self" is the guiding force behind how others are treated, and even though Jesus highlighted this rule when he said "all the Law and the Prophets hang on these two commands" (Matthew 22:40), this does not mean we must make this statement his end-all guideline for loving others. There are other Scriptural teachings that, when combined with the Golden Rule, bring a more complete picture of Christ-like love.

The Platinum Rule gets closer to Jesus' love standard, because it requires us to take the filter off our eyes and place it on the eyes of the receiver. This means we express love to others by filtering our actions through their eyes—seeing their needs from their perspective. As Philippians 2:3-4 says, "Don't be selfish; don't live to make a good impression on others. Be humble, thinking of others as better than yourself. Don't think only about your own affairs, but be interested in others, too, and what they are doing." The Platinum Rule goes further than the Golden Rule. It's the Golden Rule expanded. It says treating others the way we want to be treated is excellent, but stepping into their shoes and seeing things from their vantage point is even more excellent.

But . . .

The most excellent way is the Titanium Rule! Following it enables us to authentically love that squirrelly, seventh grade boy who has yet to discover deodorant. It's the kind of love that truly cares when the phone rings at 2 AM, and we discover one more student has gone too far. It's the most complete picture of Christ-like love!

What is the Titanium Rule? If the Golden Rule means expressing love that's filtered through my eyes, and the Platinum Rule means expressing love that's filtered through the receiver's eyes, then the Titanium Rule means expressing love that's filtered through Jesus' eyes. See why it's the most complete picture of Jesus' desire for loving others? As Len Sweet points out, "The most astonishing difference between Jesus' relationship with his disciples and other ancient teacher/student roles is finally revealed. In John 15:9, Jesus lays down what is behind what I have called 'The Jesus Commandment' or 'The Titanium Rule.' *Do unto others as I have done unto you.*"[35] Jesus' new rule, his new paradigm, breaks us out of loving others in the way we'd want to be loved or even in the way they'd want to be loved and challenges us to love them in the way Jesus loves. Sweet goes on to note, "Not only is the basis of Jesus' relationship with his disciples 'love,' but it's a love that is the same in essence and energy as the Father's love for Jesus himself. It has the power and the passion of both parental love and divine love. What Jesus now demands of his 'chosen' disciples is that they abide in this distinctive, divine love. Those who continue to abide in Jesus, therefore, are abiding in this dynamic love."[36]

Do you hear what's being said? Not only is the new standard of measurement for love treating others how Christ would treat them, but our ability to love this way only comes by abiding in Christ. No longer are we asked to love others through our own power, but we are told that Christ, who lives in us, wants to love through us! It's inside out love! As we abide in Christ, we abide in this new, dynamic love and have the ability to express it to others. This is why—even if you don't measure up to the environmental standards listed earlier—you can still effectively express affection to others. Follow the new Titanium Rule by simply allowing Christ, who lives in you, to love others through you.

living as an environmentalist

When I consider my display of ignorance in the delivery room the night my daughter was born, I both laugh and cringe. I laugh because, somewhere in my subconscious, I actually thought it was possible to stretch my daughter across the room while she was still "plugged in." I can't blame it on an epidural since my wife was the "fortunate" one to experience that pleasure. Honestly, I have no excuse; I was simply distracted by all the commotion. Everything was new. Everyone was busy. There were tons of blinking lights and weird contraptions. I got so caught up in the particulars, I missed the bigger picture.

This realization leads to why I also cringe when I think of that night. All too often, I make similar subconscious mistakes with regards to making disciples of Jesus Christ among teenagers. I have great intentions, even solid plans, for creating a loving environment, but frequently I allow myself to get distracted by all the commotion of youth ministry. Whether it is youth ministry's version of blinking lights and gadgets or just the diversion of details, my tendency is to get so caught up in the particulars that I miss the bigger picture of simply loving students.

With all the distractions, how can we be relational environmentalists who love students as Christ would love them? The answer is not in creating another program; it is in making sure we, as youth leaders, live out the Titanium Rule in our personal lives. It is in creating such a loving environment within our lives that when we rub shoulders with students, the love of Christ splashes out of us and gets them all wet.

How do we splash students with Christ-like love? Here are some practical ideas that should help.

become a meteorologist

As a relational environmentalist, one of your roles is to assess the "climate" of your ministry. What is the relational temperature of your youth group? To find out, sit down for a few minutes after your next youth gathering to consider the atmospheric markings in your group. What attitudes, emotions, and feelings did you notice? You might want to ask several students for their opinions. Give them a list of descriptions, and let them circle the five phrases they think best describe the group. Getting a proper "weather report" is a great first step toward creating an irresistible environment of love.

remember: love is a verb

"Hey, haven't ya heard, 'luv,' 'luv' is a verb." In 1992, *Free At Last* hit music store shelves and proclaimed to all the world that " 'luv' is a verb." Even though the song is dated, the words still ring as true today as when they were originally sung. As 1 John 3:18 states, "Let us stop just saying we love each other; let us really show it by our actions." And it's true, Titanium Rule love requires action. So don't refer to love as just a feeling. Act, speak, live, and teach love as a verb!

live by the *water under the bridge* principle

I'm human. Students in my ministry are human. Put humans together, and you get conflict. This isn't cynical, it's reality. Want another dose of reality? If we, as leaders, can't figure out how to forgive, then making disciples among students will be impossible. When writing to the believers in Ephesus, Paul encouraged them to live as children of Light who are kind to and compassionate with each other, forgiving one another as Christ has forgiven them (Ephesians 4:32). Students, parents, pastors, and volunteers can all say and do hurtful things. As people called to lead teenagers toward the Light, we can't afford to have clouds of unforgiveness blocking the Light's ray. Don't ignore conflict; deal with it in a Christ-like manner until you can truly say, "It's water under the bridge" (see chapter 10 for more ideas on handling conflict).

> **inside info**
>
> There's a rumor that started years ago in youth ministry that says, "Teens share more deeply with one another than adults." But research continues to disputes this claim. Granted, they do share with one another frequently, but when it comes to the deepest, most significant aspects of life, their desire is to have a trusted adult in their lives to go to for advice. H. Stephen Glenn, coauthor of Raising Self-Reliant Children in a Self-Indulgent World, states that "adolescents, left to their own devices, will always gravitate towards the oldest person they can find who will take them seriously and treat them with dignity and respect."

no favorites, please!

Few things are more devastating to a loving environment than the perception of youth workers who play favorites. It communicates that some teens are better than others. Consequently, even though you will connect better with certain students, fight the temptation to show favoritism. Treat all students with Christ-like love and affection, especially during group gatherings. Never allow yourself to be accused of favoritism.

lend an ear

One of the best compliments I ever received came from a parent who pulled me aside to thank me for spending time with her son. She said,

> ## outward action
>
> Even though you should not play favorites, you should invest in some students more than others. Jesus did! He invested in the twelve more than his other followers; and out of the twelve, there were three to whom he devoted even more of his time. However, the reason Christ invested so heavily in these people is not because he liked them more. He seems to have invested in these people because they were leaders could help him multiply his disciple-making movement.
>
> As youth leaders, we would be wise to follow Christ's example. I call it living by the "love everyone, but invest in the few" principle. How can you do this without showing favoritism?
>
> First, during regular youth group gatherings, love everyone! Don't give extra time to your "investment group" (i.e. student ministry team). Jesus didn't. When he was with the crowds, he gave himself to the crowds and his ministry team was expected to help him minister. In the same way, during youth group meetings, give yourself to all students. Even more, train ministry team members to minister to others.
>
> Second, Jesus used outside time to invest in his ministry team. Often Jesus pulled his team away for times of reflection, refreshment, and retooling. Again, follow Jesus' example. Meet with your ministry-level adults and students outside of regular youth group meetings. Try Sunday afternoons twice a month or one extra weeknight a month. Use this time to invest in these individuals so they, in turn, can invest in others.

"Matt always says you treat him like an adult." "Why does he feel that way?" I asked. "Because you don't talk at him, you talk with him *and listen*." What a good reminder that students are real people with real thoughts and emotions. Show students Christ-like care by listening well.

bag "hey there, partner"

How often do you rely on "partner," "buddy," or "man" in place of a kid's name? If there is any habit to bag, this is it! Many experts point out that teens today have an internal need to belong to a "tribe" or group more than any previous generation,[37] and a major way you can help them feel like they belong to your youth ministry "tribe" is to remember their names. Seriously, what shouts love louder than someone's name?

appropriate touches

If you've worked with teenagers for over a week, you've probably recognized how many are starved for affection. For these love-hungry kids, nothing champions Christ-like love like appropriate, physical displays of affection from genuine, caring adults. As Doug Fields says, "One of the ingredients for teenagers' emotional health is that they experience proper affection. Everyone has 'skin hunger,' and the hunger must be fed in appropriate ways. We must figure out how to touch kids in a safe manner that models Christ-like affection."[38]

However . . .

When it comes to physical touch, everyone has an opinion about what is and is not appropriate. Rather than sharing my opinion, here are a few thoughts that should help you establish your own guidelines.

First, youth workers should establish written guidelines concerning what constitutes appropriate displays of affections. These guidelines should spell what is and is not appropriate for both student-to-student touch and adult-to-student touch. Don't go nuts and write a twenty-five page document, just make the guidelines clear and easy to understand. Also, get the guidelines approved by whatever church authority exists (Governing Board, Elders, Senior Pastor, etc.) before presenting them to the youth group.

What makes this process difficult is there is a fine line between protecting people from inappropriate behavior and becoming legalistic. Most

> **inside info**
>
> There are no guarantees! Even if you set up what you consider a full-proof system for keeping inappropriate touch from occurring, it can still happen. Humans are creative in their ability to sin.
>
> Your job, then, is to establish appropriate guidelines that church leaders support, communicate the guidelines clearly, and expect people to follow them. If someone breaks the guidelines, don't punish everyone by creating over-the-top rules. Deal with the individual while continuing to champion your well thought-out plan with the rest of your team.

would agree that hand shakes, high fives, and the affirming pat on the back are fine, but what about other, more intimate touches? When addressing these more delicate matters, here are some questions to consider:

- What kind of hug is fitting? Are sideways, one-arm, shoulder hugs the only kind of hug that is appropriate, or are frontal hugs okay?
- What about backrubs or sitting on laps?
- What is your PDA rule (Public Display of Affection) between couples?

> As mature Christian leaders, we need to be able to model appropriate male/female affection. Obviously, we need to be careful here! Not only can inappropriate affection lead to inappropriate relationships, it can also send misleading and unintended messages to impressionable teenagers. I explain to my young leaders (those in their 20s) that there's a big difference between a student getting a hug from me (in my 40s, a father figured, married, my own kids in the youth group) and a hug from them.
>
> Doug Fields
> from "The Power of Affection" in
> *GROUP Magazine*,
> November/December 2005

Second, once guidelines have been established, adult leaders must clearly and regularly communicate what appropriate, loving touches look like. This means volunteers must be trained in appropriate touch and encouraged to model this behavior. Keep communicating, training, and modeling, and soon everyone will know, almost instinctively, what is and isn't acceptable.

Third, a way to almost guarantee that only appropriate touch is occurring between leaders and students is to never allow adults to spend time alone with a student of the opposite sex (some even believe this guideline should be followed with adults and students of the same sex). Practically everyone who touches others in public does so in an appropriate manner, which means this approach automatically creates a high level of protection and accountability. If there are leaders who either demonstrate inappropriate expressions of affection publicly or break the "never alone" policy, be sure to immediately address your concerns with them individually and make sure they understand there is no leniency in this area.

beware of BFF

"BFF" stands for "best friends forever." It is penned by many students at the end of notes or IMs. As cool and enticing as it may seem, youth workers should resist the urge to be "best friends" with students. The moment we cross the line and become friend first and youth worker second, we blur our authority role and lose the ability to inspire, confront, and challenge. This is not to say we cannot be friends, it just means that when friction between the two roles occurs, the youth worker role must win out. You are a youth leader first, a friend second.

take me to your leader

Finally, students will remember a lot from their days in youth ministry. Hopefully, one memory at the top of their list will be how you demonstrated Jesus' love through your life. According to 1 John 4:12, "No one has ever seen God," yet if we practice Titanium Rule love, students will see Christ's love flowing from within us through our actions. If you want to create an irresistible environment of love that enhances your ability to make disciples of Jesus Christ, use your life to take students to your leader.

where's your passion?

I love baseball! Every spring, the smell of fresh cut grass reminds me of countless days I spent on the diamond—fielding ground balls and taking batting practice. If a Major League team offered me a chance to play, even for a Single A team, I would drop everything. Baseball is in my blood!

Passion is a funny thing. It can drive people to new heights and achievements, but it can also lead to obsessions. Take me, for instance. My passion for baseball borders on obsession. No amount of baseball bores me. I can watch games and highlights on TV all day long, spend gobs of money traveling to different ballparks, and fiddle with my fantasy team for hours. You could say baseball consumes me.

I sometimes wonder if God is disappointed in the priority of my passions. The contrast between my passion for an utterly meaningless thing like baseball and my passion for making disciples among teenagers is, at times, disgusting. I wonder what goes through the mind of God when He looks at my wandering heart. My lips may mouth love words about God to students, but my life doesn't always back up what I'm saying.

Yet, I am committed to making disciples among students, and deep down, I am passionately committed to creating an irresistible atmosphere of love within my life and ministry. Day-by-day, my prayer is that Titanium Love will become as much of an obsession for me as my compulsion for baseball.

My prayer is the same for you! I pray that you become obsessed with the Titanium Rule, that you strive to be a relational environmentalist, that your inside passion for Christ would splash out and soak teenagers, and that Christ-like love would be a lifeline for students in your ministry.

inside out questions

1. Do you consider yourself a "relational environmentalist?" Why or why not?

2. Which environmental DNA qualities are evident in how you express love for teenagers? Give examples.

   - Advocate
   - Watchdog
   - Recruiter
   - Influencer

3. Which description best describes how you express love to others? Why?

   - The Golden Rule
   - The Platinum Rule
   - The Titanium Rule

4. Which of the practical ideas for creating an atmosphere of affection in your group are you currently practicing? Which would you like to implement?

5. Why is the work of affection so crucial to making disciples of Jesus Christ among teenagers?

the work of CONTACTING

by Erik (w/a "k") Williams

Contact work is lifestyle, not just a technique...

Young Life Leadership Website

One of the scariest things I've ever done as a youth worker is walk onto a middle school campus. No lie! Even though I'm an extrovert, I totally freaked the first time I ventured onto a campus. I had flashbacks of when I was in middle school. I remembered having no idea where the office was, wondering if I would see anyone I knew (a major fear), and hoping to be accepted by someone (a mammoth fear).

This time, I was 25 years old and about to try my hand at "contacting" students. I had geared myself up to be a shining light in a really, really dark world—all the while, preparing myself to be mocked, picked on, and made fun of—much like when I was in middle school. As I timidly walked through the doors, the first thing I noticed was the smell. Sort of a pepperoni, sweaty gym socks odor mixed with an awful lot of gaudy preteen perfume. The aroma hadn't changed. Gross, but ahhh . . . familiar. In a weird sort of way, it felt good. It didn't smell good, but it felt good.

I found the office, filled out the proper paperwork, and began the long journey down the hall to whatever fate awaited me. Just then, the bell rang, doors flew open, and a river of humanity began flowing around me at chest level. Within seconds, I heard my name shouted from the other end of the hallway. Becca, Laura, and Julianne screamed as they ran to greet me. Ahhh, I was feeling even better. Soon a group of eight students who went to my church were hangin' out with me. They couldn't believe I was there to see them; I couldn't believe they were so excited to see me. Ahhh, more good vibes.

But therein was the dilemma. I liked knowing that students at a particular school were excited to see me. It felt good. I could visit whenever I needed an ego stroke. But what about other schools? I didn't think much about it at the time, but in the back of my mind . . .

A week later, I strolled onto another middle school campus. My swagger was confident, perhaps even cocky. As I walked through the doors, the initial indicators led me to believe I was in store for another positive experience. I signed in, smelled that familiar smell, and started down the hallway. It felt good; yet in an instant, everything changed. I spotted Josiah. He looked at me quizzically and asked, "What are you doing here?" I enthusiastically said, "I came to hang out with you!" With confusion and a hint of disgust, he grunted back, "Why?"

At that moment, I realized my incentive for contacting couldn't be about an ego boost, because it wasn't going to happen on every occasion. It might even be more rare than common. Deep down, I knew contacting was about students; but honestly, I wasn't sure I could keep at it without the good feeling I initially experienced.

why contact?

Contacting could be defined as getting out of the church setting and connecting with students on their turf. It's that simple. But let's face it, most youth workers, even inside out youth workers who are committed to making disciples, struggle with contacting. We love students and enjoy hangin' with them, as long as the place is comfortable *for us*. But try hangin' out with students *on their turf*—school, the student section during a football game, a food joint that's packed with high schoolers, or anyplace where there is a 20-1 teen-to-adult ratio. These are unfamiliar, uncomfortable terrains—at least at first, and they can make us feel like we are in a foreign country with bizarre customs.

So why contact? If it's so uncomfortable, why can't we just expect students to meet us? Is it really necessary to step outside the church setting? Absolutely!

The reasons for contacting are numerous. For instance, contacting:

- demonstrates love and concern;
- provides a chance for relationships to grow deeper;
- helps youth workers get a glimpse of teenagers' real world;
- helps students see youth workers as real people, and
- creates memories and life-changing moments.

But these reasons, as well as the others that could be listed, are not the "big why." The true reason for contacting teenagers is Jesus! We contact students to help them see Jesus better, fall in love with him, follow him, and enjoy him forever. This doesn't happen through contacting alone, but contacting plays a huge role in creating an environment for Jesus to transform students.

We also contact because Jesus did it himself. He stepped onto our turf when He joined us here on earth. In fact, his coming fulfilled all the bullet points listed above and a bunch of others:

- it demonstrated God's divine love and concern for us;
- it restored the relationship we had bankrupted with God, and
- by taking on bodily form, Jesus didn't simply gain a glimpse of human reality, he experienced it. He felt it, touched it, smelled it, and tasted it as a human, just like us.

In other words, through the incarnation, we didn't experience a "less filling, taste great" version of God Almighty, we saw "in Christ the fullness of God living in a human body" (Colossians 2:9) and "the radiance of God's glory and the exact representation (imprint) of his being" (Hebrews 1:3 NIV). Every iota of the completeness of God dwelt in Jesus (Colossians 1:19), so seeing Jesus is the same as seeing the Father (John 14:9).

Are you catching what is being said? *Contacting is all about Jesus!*

If you're like me, you probably find this "big why" stirring, even inspiring, but it doesn't necessarily make contacting any easier. When I read the gospels, it's cool to see people screaming Jesus' name "from down the hallway." But what about the "what are you doing here" stories? I'm not a big fan of those. But as Jesus warned us, "Do you remember what I told you? 'A servant is not greater than the master.' Since they persecuted me, naturally they will persecute you" (John 15:20a).

So even though the "big why" doesn't necessarily make contacting easier, it does make it more meaningful. Just knowing that contacting was a principle in the life of Christ gives me courage to step outside my comfort zone and onto the turf of teenagers. Likewise, knowing Jesus' final challenge included contacting moves me to action. "I have been given complete authority in heaven and on earth. Therefore, go and make disciples of all the nations, baptizing them in the name of the Father and the Son and the Holy Spirit. Teach these new disciples to obey all the commands I have given you. And be sure of this: I am with you always, even to the end of the age" (Matthew 28:18b-20). As Kent said in the first chapter, the command here is to "make disciples," but one of the key action steps is to "go." This means that if I am to make disciples, I must go. Go . . . and intentionally get onto students' turf. Go . . . and rub shoulders with students. Go . . . and love students. Go . . . and pray for open doors. Go . . . and share Jesus with students. Go . . . and see what happens. Go . . . and know Jesus is with me. Go! Go! Go!

Bottom line, "going" helps inside out youth workers make disciples because it earns them the right to be heard. The more time youth workers spend with a student on his turf, investing in a genuine, caring friendship, the more they'll get to know that student and the more he'll get to know them. Through contacting, a relationship is poised for growth.

You might argue with this next point, but reality is Jesus used contacting to earn the right to be heard. It wasn't a technique or formula; it is just the way he was. He initiated relationships! He could have shouted the good news from heaven, but he didn't. He, the Good News, came to our turf so we could know him and the Father better.

True, Jesus didn't need to "earn" anything; he is God, for goodness sake. Lord of Lords! King of Kings! As Don Everts writes, "At his word he could command all attention and obedience. He is Lord over all. That is not fodder for a worship song—that is reality. He is Lord over everything. His authority knows no bounds."[39] Still, Jesus chose to come. "Though he was God, he did not demand and cling to his rights as God. He made himself nothing; he took the humble position of a slave and appeared in human form" (Philippians 2:6-7). That's earning the right to be heard. That's contacting! May our "attitude be the same as Christ Jesus" (Philippians 2:5).

be you!

Realizing that contacting is all about Jesus should make you want to break out of the "church-only" world and get onto students' turf. But before getting into specifics about how to contact, let's be clear about one thing. When contacting students, be you! Don't try to be Joe-youth-guy or Jodie-youth-girl. Students have an innate ability to see past false fronts, so don't do it—you'll be found out.

Even if you weren't found out, of what value is a fake you? I guarantee you'll have less impact if you try to be someone you're not. Just be you! Don't get suckered into buying tons of new apparel so you can be "cool." Stop worrying about whether you know the latest teenage lingo. And beware of acting like a kid in an attempt to be relevant. As Doug Fields recently wrote, "Teenagers aren't looking for a twentysomething, cool, well-dressed, culturally-relevant, extrovert who will skateboard with them. Instead, they want someone who will care about them, listen to them, and possibly watch them skateboard. It's very clear they're looking for meaningful relationships more than superficial relevance."[40]

I agree with Doug—a relationship is more important than relevance.

In fact, a relationship equals relevance! God has designed you exactly the way you are so that you can reach specific students, and part of the reason you were put here on earth was to reach the certain students that only you, through Christ, can reach. Sure, some students will flat out reject you—it's like that for all of us. But others will accept you and even be drawn to you. Your job is to be you. Allow God to do his job and use you in whomever he desires.

Okay, onto the details of contacting . . .

what to say?

I've seen big, tough guys freak when they walk onto a school campus because they simply don't know what to talk about with teenagers. Honestly, I'm talking chilled to the bone anxiety. So don't worry if you get nervous about what to say. Everyone does. I know I do.

time speaks volumes

Before getting too worked up about what to talk about, keep in mind that your time probably speaks louder than your words. You simply can't put a price tag on spending time with students on their turf. When you show up at school, a special event, or any other place of importance to students, you show you care. Teenagers realize, at least on a subconscious level, that you have gone out of your way to be with them. Even when students don't seem to care (sorry, but it will happen), you are still making an impact. What other adult is coming to see them on their turf? They might demonstrate disinterest, but your presence won't go unnoticed, and God can use it to soften even the hardest of hearts. I've seen it too often to discount—time speaks louder than words.

F.R.I.E.S.

The best way to deal with the "what do I talk about" jitters is to actually have something to say. There are lots of "tricks" to help initiate and sustain conversations and one of my favorites is the F.R.I.E.S. method.

It's easy to remember, especially since teenagers love munching on french fries. Here's the gist of F.R.I.E.S.

Friends. Saying friends are important to teenagers is like saying oxygen is important for breathing, so it makes sense to ask tons of questions about friends. Find out who their friends are and what they're like. What do they do with their friends? Where do they go? How do they spend their time? If you get the chance, get to know their friends. Students will feel more accepted by you when they see you showing genuine interest in their friends.

Relatives. For years, I thought peers were the most influential people in the lives of teenagers (like I said, they're as important as oxygen). Imagine my surprise when I discovered most research indicates that there is a group of people even more important than friends. Parents! In study after study, parents rank as the most influential people in teenagers' lives.[41] For this reason, it makes sense to find out about teens' parents and family. What do they appreciate about their parents? Do both parents live at home? How many siblings do they have? What do they like doing together as a family? What's a favorite family memory or trip? As my relationships grow deeper, I've asked if they get along with their parents or who they connect with best and why. Also, just for fun, since many teens consider pets to be part of the family, I ask about their pet. It's a good way to bring up a lighthearted topic.

As an FYI, some students will let you know they can't stand spending time with their parents. Don't be afraid to explore that a bit. Depending on your relationship, you can get into some fairly substantial stuff. Be careful, though, of trying to solve family problems or taking sides. In most cases, it's best just to listen.

Interests. What do they do in their free time? What gets their crank turning (don't use this phrase, because they won't have a clue what you're talking about)? Once you discover a special interest, ask more specific questions. How did they get into it? Why do they like it so much? Do they see themselves doing something with this interest in the future? If you discover a common interest, you now have a topic to come back to frequently. Perhaps it's even something you can do together with them and their friends.

Extra-curricular activities. These activities go beyond interests and usually involve organized groups. For instance, are students involved in sports? How about band? Drama? Singing? Debate? Martial arts? How'd they get involved? Why do they enjoy it? Any other activities they want to try? Again, if you find an activity you have in common, you have something to talk about and perhaps do together. Plus, whether you're interested in the extra-curricular activity or not, going to watch students do their thing always makes them feel valued.

Story. What's their story? Where were they born? Where did they grow up? What schools have they attended? Where else have they lived? Do they have a favorite childhood story? What do they think about some of the big topics of our day? You can even ask about their spiritual story. I typically ask how God fits into their life, if at all. Asking this question usually comes up naturally in the midst of conversations about these other things, and most teens are willing to share quite a bit if sincere interest is shown.

There you go—F.R.I.E.S. You are now armed with some decent conversation starters. Onto the next question—where do you go? What constitutes students' turf?

where to go?

The largest teenage turfs in most communities are middle schools and high schools. Students invest the majority of their time there, so it

> **inside info**
>
> At most public schools, visitors are not allowed to start "spiritual" conversations, so find out the laws in your school district and abide by them. In most cases, it's best to view a campus visit as an opportunity to build relationship, not as a means for being a verbal witness. However, remember the big picture! Giving a verbal witness is an important part of evangelism, but it's not the only part. Building meaningful relationships is just as significant. If you view school visits through these lenses, you'll realize how significant visits are to the disciple-making process—even if you don't verbally talk about Christ.

> ### inside info . . . a true story
>
> I was asked to join several others from the "faith community" in our town to hear about a government-sponsored after-school program called POWER. During the meeting, we were told schools were in desperate need of volunteers and most were open to discuss practically any idea we could dream up. I leaned over to the guy next to me and said, "It would be awesome to teach break-dancing." Yeah, dream on!
>
> A month later, I received a phone call from a parent in our church. I'll spare you the details, but the gist of the story is that she asked if I would be interested in teaching break-dancing at a school I visited frequently. I ended up teaching every Monday afternoon for three years. What a contacting opportunity!
>
> On a side note, I loved reminding my mom of the time she told me, "Break-dancing is just a fad. Why waste your time? You'll never use it when you get older."

makes sense to try to hang out on this turf as much as possible. Some school districts are opened to visitors, while others are not. I have personally experienced both.

getting onto campus . . .

As a youth pastor in the Atlanta-area, I thought I would be welcomed like a king (I was in the buckle of the Bible-belt, or so I thought). During the first few months of school, I just showed up and met students outdoors during lunch. When it started getting cold, I went inside and saw a sign that read, "All Visitors Must Report to the Main Office." Who knew? I went to the office and found out that no visitors were allowed on campus unless accompanied by a parent. Naturally, that ended my campus visitations in Atlanta (at least at public schools).

A few years later, I moved to Oregon. My preliminary understanding of the school culture in the Pacific Northwest was it wasn't very open to church workers. My experience, however, has proved otherwise. The school district actually wanted me around!

Each school I have visited over the years has had it own idiosyncrasies, but most have been pretty welcoming. I've invested the majority of my energies into the handful of schools where most my students attend since a key to long-term success in contacting is consistency. This has allowed students, as well as school administrators and teachers, to get to know and trust me. Amazingly, once staff people knew me, they'd thank me for coming and go out of their way to let me know I was welcome anytime. In one particular school, I asked the administrators if they had any needs. Before I could blink, I was chaperoning school dances and field trips. I was even asked to counsel students after a shooting occurred. Again, the trust level, over time, had become outstanding.

What do you do if your school district is not open to visitors during the day or if your schedule prohibits you from visiting during school hours? No worries, there are still lots of opportunities for contacting students at school. Sporting events, school plays, concerts, musicals, graduations, and career days are just a few ways to connect.

outward action

A way to get involved in schools that are "closed" to visitors is to volunteer. Check your motives—don't volunteer just to work around the system. If you truly desire to serve, then volunteering might be a great opportunity for you to contact students while serving. Some schools (especially middle schools) are likely to use volunteers in the following ways:

- Helping with lunch duty
- Serving as a hall monitor
- Working as a janitor
- Coaching a sports team
- Facilitating a school club
- Helping with after school programs
- Chaperoning field trips or school dances
- Making video highlights for sporting events, plays, concerts, etc.
- Helping with student registration
- Tutoring

once on campus . . .

Wondering what to do after you sign in at the office? Here are a few ideas. First, let students from your youth ministry know ahead of time that you are coming. This at least gives you someone to look for. Once you connect, there are many options. I usually hang out in the lunchroom and make my rounds by popping from table to table. I'll also check out the "commons" area, gym, or ball field. The gym and ball field are a huge hang out for middle school boys. They love to shoot hoops, play bump, or throw the football.

When meeting new students, it is very important to learn and *remember* names. You may use the excuse I once did and say you don't have a good memory for names (nice try), but if a person's name is the most important word in his or her vocabulary, then being a good contactor requires learning and using students' names.

So what can you do to remember names better? Be intentional! You don't have to stay awake until 1:00 AM and order a mega-memory program off an infomercial, just keep 3x5 cards or your Palm Pilot with you to write down names and descriptions of students you meet. I record names in a special file on my Palm Pilot and write as many details as I can about a person to have a better frame of reference next time I talk to him or her. The first time I remembered to briefly review this file before going back to a particular school, I was able to go up to a student and ask about his mom's surgery. He couldn't believe I remembered. He hardly remembered me, but after that, he went out of his way to talk with me.

off campus . . .

There are other places besides school where you can connect with students. If students have jobs, visit them at work. Don't take up their time (you'll get them fired), just stop in and say "hi." You can even drop off an encouragement card or their favorite candy bar to brighten their day (they'll definitely look forward to your visits if you do this). You can even be a patron of students' workplaces. I like to eat at restaurants where my students serve and request to have them serve me. After the meal, I leave a good tip, along with a positive comment on the comment card. My students score big points with management!

Youth hang-out spots like parks, pools, the mall, coffee shops, and skate parks are other places to contact students. There is a place near me called "The Hoop." Tons of teens play basketball there, and six or eight games are usually going on at once. I show up, and in one shot, I connect with a bunch of students and any parents who happen to be watching. Sometimes I play, and other times, I bring along my digital camera. In twenty minutes, I have enough pictures for a slide show on Sunday. So whether you play sports or not, you can still hang out with students in venues like this.

One other great place to contact students is in their homes. This is the ultimate student turf. You'll discover a ton about teenagers by seeing where they live and how they interact with family.

When meeting a teen in his home, it's important to remember a few things. First, never meet a student at home alone; make sure other family members are around. In fact, I don't visit unless an adult is present, it's just common sense. Second, it is best to have a decent relationship with a student before considering this kind of contact. You are stepping into personal territory here, so tread lightly. Third, don't just show up. Most parents want their home looking presentable for company, even casual company. Therefore, make a courtesy call first.

There are many advantages of visiting students at home. You get to see how they live, develop relationships with other family mem-

> **outward action**
>
> Here are some ideas of things to do and places to go.
>
> - Bowling
> - Play pool
> - Laser tag
> - Swimming
> - White water rafting
> - Pickup basketball
> - Rollerblading or skateboarding
> - Surfing
> - Frisbee or disc golf
> - Golf
> - Watch the movie *Napoleon Dynamite* (see who can quote the most lines)
> - Miniature golf
> - Window shopping

bers, and if you're lucky, get invited over for meals (yum, free food). You get to know students on a level that won't occur through other venues and will see first hand what they are going through (e.g. relationship with their parents, how parents treat them, where they fall in the food chain with siblings, etc.).

> ### outward action–for ladies only
>
> Here are a few thoughts from Melinda Lankford, the only female author in this book, on contacting girls:
>
> - Girls love going to lunch, dinner, or coffee.
> - Shopping, sleepovers, and TPing (note: TPing is not officially endorsed by the authors of this book) always get conversations flowing.
> - Finding out the "secret" guy a girl likes gives you a springboard for sharing what God wants in dating.
> - It's OK to be into fashion—unique purses, cute clothes, or cool sunglasses—because fashion makes for a good conversation starter.
> - Remember, you are NOT a teenager, so don't be intimidated if "popular" girls don't seem to like you (guy youth workers just don't get this). Be consistent in how you treat everyone. Even "snooty" girls will likely come around if you show true interest in them and don't stoop to their level of pettiness.
> - Make phone calls—girls love the phone!
> - Mail cards—again, girls love this!
> - Play to your strengths. Are you young and hip? Play to it. Are you dating? Girls love talking about boyfriends—teach them Godly principles through their interest in your romance. Are you a mom? Bring your kids with you when contacting. Are you a grandma? Be the person girls always come to for a hug.

There is also a ton to do during a home visit. This might sounds obvious, but often youth workers show up, sit down, and do the small talk thing. Instead, help with homework, play a board game, shoot hoops, throw the football, scrapbook, or play video games.

the big picture

Contacting isn't about connecting with students once a month or even once a week. It's a lifestyle! For inside out youth workers who are committed to making disciples of Jesus Christ, it needs to be part of who we are at our core, not just something we do while wearing our "youth leader" hat. This means contacting other people besides students. For instance, when you go grocery shopping, go to the same store regularly. Learn your checker's and bagger's names. Talk to them. I regularly go to Roth's grocery store, and one of my favorite people there is a cashier named Carole. She's so helpful and is always smiling. I've often told her that she is the reason I shop at Roth's. This always makes her day and leads to a nice conversation. It's just one way I make contacting a lifestyle.

I also go to the same Starbucks even though I am not a coffee drinker. I get my "grande" (that's medium size for those who don't speak Starbuck-ese) caramel apple cider and usually talk with Sasha. She's been working there for quite some time, and we chat about common friends and the latest happenings on certain reality shows. Sasha has met my family, and I've met hers.

There is just something to being a patron at the same places on a regular basis—shopping at the same grocery store, getting your gas at the same gas station, and picking up your coffee at the same coffee shop. If you are intentional, always looking to build relationships and always praying, you just never know what will happen. At an unexpected moment in an unexpected place, you'll have an opportunity to be Christ's light in your community.

Thinking about this kind of intentionality brings us back to Philippians 2. Jesus came to serve and contacting was one of the greatest, most practical ways he served. So our "attitude should be the same that Christ Jesus had. Though he was God, he did not demand and cling to his rights as God. He made himself nothing; he took the humble position of a slave and appeared in human form. And in human form, he obediently humbled himself even further by dying a criminal's death on a cross"

(Philippians 2:5-8). Being a servant is what contacting is all about. Our conversations, intentional relationships, and visits to schools are all about serving. When I think of Jesus, I imagine what he would do to contact the students I know. I imagine him going to see Molly and Sheena performing in their eighth grade play and enjoying every minute of it. I imagine him hanging out with Toby and Josh at lunch or shooting baskets with Joey and Ryan at The Hoop. I imagine him sharing stories with Sasha at Starbucks. All and all, I imagine him doing the same sort of things I'm trying to do . . . and that makes me feel pretty good!

just do it!

I hate to end with a slogan, but there's no better challenge when it comes to contacting than *Just Do It*! Don't wait for someone to ask you to visit him or her at school. Don't wait for your youth pastor to ask you to hang out with students. Just go do it. Get out there and get it done. Go! This chapter may help with ideas, but ultimately, you need to follow through and do it. In fact, the very best thing you can do right now is put down this book and contact students. If it's lunchtime, get on a campus. If it's after school, call up a student and go hang out. If you are nervous, take someone with you. You can do it! You don't need more training. Go and be the bright shining light Jesus wants you to be. You're ready, so just do it!

inside out questions

1. Define contacting in your own words.

2. Give three reasons why contacting is so important to making disciples of Jesus Christ among teenagers.

3. Do you like contacting? Why or why not?

4. Are you good at contacting? Why or why not?

5. Do you find it difficult to "be you" when contacting students? Why or why not?

6. What contacting strategies have worked well for you?

7. What new contacting ideas did you gain from this chapter that you would like to try? How will you implement them?

8. How can you make contacting a lifestyle?

10 — the work of RESOLUTION

by John Zivonjinovic

Peace is not the absence of conflict but the presence of creative alternatives for responding to conflict.

Dorothy Thompson

Several years ago at a summer camp, I entered a room that was housing our junior high guys. In true middle school fashion, they greeted me with full moons. I laughed it off, said what needed to be said, and as I left, I dropped my shorts and flashed a quick moon of my own. It was only a quarter-moon, mind you, but they got the message. I chuckled and didn't think any more of it.

Within days of returning from camp, several moms called to express their utter disgust at my quarter-moon. Having been in student ministry for twenty years, I realized that mooning is a guy tradition—sort of a rite of passage—so I was thrown off a bit by their responses. I soon discovered, however, that this was a big deal to these ladies. One mom had talked to ten others, and then she phoned my Executive Pastor to call for my immediate dismissal. I actually spent two hours on the phone with another lady as she expressed her anguish over my "immoral" behavior.

By this point, my frustration was at an all-time high, so I asked her for chapter and verse from the Bible to justify her accusation. This, of course, only stoked her anger. Realizing I wasn't getting anywhere, I tried to end the conversation gently with the "let's just agree to disagree" approach. She didn't bite. It was clear that she was only going to hang up when she was good and ready to hang up, and I felt obligated to stay on the phone rather than risk exacerbating the situation. Eventually my Executive Pastor bailed me out of the whole mess, but it took two months for the dust to settle.

On another occasion, I was in a deep conversation with a guy who was struggling through some sexual issues. A female adult leader overheard one sentence of our conversation, and based on that single sentence, became extremely upset with me. After struggling with her feelings for a week, she stopped by to see me and was clearly angry. "What's up?" I asked. Those words barely escaped my mouth before she unleashed her wrath, telling me that my words to the young man were both inappropriate and unnecessary. When I asked how she came across the information, she informed me that she had passed by the high school room during my conversation with this young man. "Did you hear the entire conversation?" She answered no. As I filled her in, she recognized that her reaction was based on a misunderstood fragment of the exchange. Oops!

> *The art of living is more like wrestling than dancing.*
>
> Marcus Aurelius
> Roman emperor and stoic

One other story . . . my Senior Pastor, one of five with whom I have served, was addressing an issue at a Christian Education meeting. At one point, I spoke up and said, "You told me last week you did not like this because . . ." It would be an understatement to say he was upset. I had inadvertently tipped his hand and exposed an issue he had wanted to present with much more tact and diplomacy. After everyone left, he chewed me out—rightfully and deservedly—and I stood there, feeling like a worm.

These three vignettes represent just a few examples of the many conflicts I've experienced in ministry. Each time I face conflict, the first thought that pops into my mind is, "Houston, we have a problem." Remember that movie? In *"Apollo 13,"* when Jim Lovell (played by Tom Hanks) uttered those famous words, from that point on, the problems NASA and the three astronauts of Apollo 13 faced were literally "out of this world." Yet, the "Houston, we have a problem" thought doesn't discourage me. If you remember the movie, you'll remember that each out-of-this-world problem was recognized, responded to, and resolved. So, for me, saying "Houston, we have a problem" is simply the first step in the process of dealing with conflict—it's recognizing that there is a conflict.

In ministry, you can count on conflict. It's going to happen! Some conflicts will be simple to resolve—others, not so much. This chapter looks at conflict and addresses how to be a good steward of it both personally and in ministry. In other words, it's all about inside out youth workers being able to say with confidence, "Houston, we have a problem."

recognizing conflict

The ability to properly recognize conflict is the first step in dealing with it confidently. This means inside out youth workers must be able to define conflict and recognize its various expressions in youth ministry.

defining conflict

Conflict can be defined as, "any situation in which two or more social entities or 'parties' . . . perceive that they possess mutually incompatible goals."[42] For this discussion, I will define conflict as any disagreement, impasse, positional struggle, or dispute that arises within oneself or between one individual and another (or others). By its very nature, conflict is global, but this chapter will focus only on intra-personal, inter-personal, intra-group, inter-group, and congregational conflict.

Intra-personal conflict. This is conflict that arises within oneself.

When struggling with a serious decision or moral judgment, individuals wrestle inwardly by struggling with themselves about the decision.

Inter-personal conflict. Inter-personal conflict takes place between one person and another. For example, a parent may approach you with the concern that her teen is "not fitting in" at youth group and express an expectation that you "fix" the situation. When you explain that her daughter doesn't seem to want to "fit in" and refuses to talk to others, even when they try to talk to her; if your words fall on deaf ears and the mother continues to insist that you get her daughter "plugged in," this becomes an inter-personal conflict. It happens frequently with students, parents, elders, church members, and fellow youth workers.

Intra-group conflict. This kind of conflict arises when there are factions within a group. Perhaps some members of a small group want to spend group time in conversation, while others want to study the Bible. Frustration develops as group members perceive mutually incompatible goals. Ultimately, the more outspoken members tend to determine the environment. The problem is usually not resolved, however, since one faction has simply dictated the structure for the entire group.

Inter-group conflict. Inter-group conflict happens between groups. In youth ministry, this could surface as rivalry between students from different high schools or perhaps a disagreement between the Christian education board and the elder board.

Congregational conflict. The granddaddy of them all, congregational conflict, exists when there is pervasive tension among church attendees. In extreme situations, a congregation splits over the conflict and the perceived minority group leaves or starts another church. Painful splits have occurred over seemingly insignificant issues such as which side of the pulpit the piano should be on, carpet color choice, or the traditional hymns vs. contemporary songs debate. Other splits have been over more substantive issues such as biblical doctrine or purpose of ministry.

Now that we have defined conflict and looked at its various expressions in ministry, a few more observations are necessary in order to get a more complete picture.

scripture talks about conflict

Most individuals portrayed in Scripture experienced conflict. Think of Adam and Eve's disobedience toward God, Cain's murder of Abel, Pharaoh's conflict with Moses, King Saul with David, Israel and the pagan nations, David and Goliath, Mordecai and Haman, Daniel and the commissioners, Hosea and Gomer, Jonah's conflict with God, Jesus and the religious leaders, the Hellenistic Jews' conflict with native Jews over feeding widows, Saul's conflict with the early Church, Paul's conflict with Barnabas concerning John Mark, the conflict of immorality in the Corinthian Church, doctrinal problems in the Colossian Church, laziness in the Thessalonian Church, the Apostle John's conflict with Gnostic theology, and the great conflict between the armies of heaven and hell that is yet to come. Dilemmas, disagreements, wars, struggles, and divine conflicts are pervasive throughout Scripture. If Scripture doesn't shy away from addressing conflict, it's in our best interest to do likewise. Additionally, a comprehensive study of Scripture is one of the best training tools available for dealing with conflict.

conflict can arise over the littlest things

I wish I could say every conflict you will face will be substantive and meaningful. The sad truth, however, is that conflict is often petty and mean-spirited. Yet, it's important to remember that every conflict, no matter how minor, is significant to the person who initiates it. Most people are not brutish and difficult; most initiate conflict from a sincere belief that their stance is right and should be heeded. This means it is important not to trivialize any conflict, no matter how inconsequential it seems.

conflict can be destructive

If conflict is not addressed properly, it can be a very destructive force in Satan's arsenal. Feelings get hurt, people are marginalized, integrity is compromised, reputations are soiled, and Christ is grieved. Conflict must not be allowed to work insidiously among us; it must be responded to appropriately.

conflict can be healthy

Conflict cannot be avoided; it's part of life. Consequently, we need to see the positive side of conflict and learn to regard it as an opportunity instead of a problem. For example, I advise pre-marital couples to see conflict as an opportunity for growth—both individually and relationally. When a spouse risks expressing opinions, feelings, and perspectives—if handled correctly by both individuals—the marriage is strengthened. In any conflict situation, taking the high road by wading through the words and personal attacks to get to the core issue is much healthier than taking the low road of avoidance or gossip. Taking the high road leads to beneficial change, traveling the low road leads to just more of the same.

In summary, conflict is guaranteed in life. Leaders should learn to recognize conflict and even see it as an opportunity for growth. Such an approach is the first step to properly dealing with conflict.

responding to conflict

The second step in dealing with conflict is to realize the different ways people respond to it. In 1978, William Wilmot proposed five conflict styles: avoid, compete, compromise, accommodate, and collaborate.[43] Below is a brief description of each.

conflict styles

The avoiding style. This style is understood as the process whereby one deals with conflict by evading it. Avoiders change the subject, try to laugh it off, become quiet, or employ other means to steer clear of conflict. They are willing to forego their needs and the needs of their disputing party to shun conflict.

The competing style. The person who employs this style wants to win at all costs. Competitors see themselves as always being in the right,

> ### outward action
>
> Intimidation, manipulation, and aggression are unacceptable conflict strategies. It should go without saying that any form of physical aggression in a dispute is absolutely wrong. Verbal intimidation and manipulation, though less dramatic, are no more acceptable. This means if someone in authority over you is trying to intimidate or manipulate you, you should immediately address the issue and even consider leaving your position. People who employ such tactics have probably followed the pattern for years and are very unlikely to change. In all probability, things will only get worse.
>
> If you are prone to intimidating and manipulating to get your way, seek professional counseling immediately. You have a problem—get help!

which means they can be aggressive, condescending, and manipulative in order to win a dispute. Conflicts are resolved quickly when the competitive style is used.

The compromising style. Compromising is the strategy that seeks to split the difference 50-50. Compromisers are willing to give a little, if they can get a little. They suspend some of their needs, but must have other needs met.

The accommodating style. Accommodators give in to the other party. Accommodators usually employ a martyr complex to feel they have gained something from a conflict when, in actuality, they have not.

The collaborating style. Collaboration is the strategy that seeks a win/win solution. Collaborators look for alternate ways to resolve conflict that leave both parties believing their needs have been met.

There are difficulties inherent in each style. *Avoiders* allow needs and concerns to go unmet because of their unwillingness to deal with conflict. *Competitors* often frustrate the disputing parties due to their aggressive approach. *Compromisers* tend to split the difference too quickly, causing both parties to feel as though they were not heard or that their needs were not completely met. *Accommodators* often feel used and exploited, despite the fact that such feelings are their own doing. *Collaborators* need time, energy, and concerted effort to reach win/win resolutions; such realities do not always exist.

Based on the brief descriptions above, is there a particular style or two that fits you? Have you observed other styles being used by people you know? Understanding your style(s), as well as the style(s) of others, enhances your ability to resolve conflict. In fact, learning the particulars of each style gives you the aptitude to face practically any situation.

communication is key

Communication is essential to any relationship, so it is not surprising that it is also the key component to traversing the rugged terrain of conflict. Conflict is often generated by a lack of good communication which, in turn, means that good communication is the basis for healthy resolution. There are numerous factors involved in communication, but five are particularly relevant in responding to conflict.

> **inside info**
>
> Although collaboration seems to be the best approach, it should be noted that each conflict style has value and can be employed in certain situations for successful resolution.
>
> For a fuller understanding, including a self-test on conflict styles, check out *Communication and Conflict Resolution Skills* by Neil H. Katz & John W. Lawyer (Dubuque, IA: Kendall/Hunt Publishing Company, 1985).

Communication hazards. Remember the old adage, "Actions speak louder than words?" It's true—people's actions communicate more than their words. Therefore, becoming skilled at interpreting actions and body language is just as important as understanding words when it comes to good communication. Even more important is learning to be careful with your own body language. Actions that break down communication include getting up and leaving, sighing, looking at a watch, yawning, slumping over, looking around the room, rolling eyes, tapping a foot or hand, interrupting, becoming visibly angry, crossing arms, or closing eyes. These actions are communication killers. Spoken words that are prideful, judgmental, arrogant, hateful, unkind, short, uncaring, angry, manipulative, begrudging, and spiteful will also unravel meaningful conversation. The bottom line is that proper words *and* actions are important.

Priorities of communication. Robert Bolton writes of three essentials to good communication: genuineness, non-possessive love, and empathy. Each priority is worth careful consideration.

"Genuineness means being what one really is without front or façade."[44] In other words, *genuineness* means authenticity. When a person puts on a front, he often compromises core values and beliefs. Such compromises result in frustration because a person knows when he is not being real with people. He might even take this frustration out on the other party. In contrast, genuineness takes courage, commitment, self-awareness, self-acceptance, and self-expression. Notice the emphasis on self; genuineness begins on the inside. One cannot be genuine on the outside if he is not first authentic on the inside.

Non-possessive love is love which causes a person to respect, appreciate, and accept another person for who they are.[45] This idea is expressed in the Greek word *agape*, used in the Bible to illustrate the selfless nature of God's unconditional love. The more someone truly loves people for who they are, the better that person's communication. Why? He has developed appreciation and respect for others.

Most people's tendency, however, is to turn others into victims of conditional love. Only when others meet their expectations do they grace people with their acceptance. Bolton points out that communication cannot be free and fluid if people are held hostage to the constraints of such conditional love. For example, a person in ministry who practices selfish love will have little influence in the lives of others. No matter what words he uses, his actions will scream, "I don't accept you!" If this same person learns to accept others unconditionally (i.e. non-possessive love), not only will his influence grow, but his communication will become more open and flowing.

Empathy is "the ability to understand another person pretty much as he understands himself. Empathetic people are able to 'crawl into another's skin' and see the world through his eyes."[46] This skill of viewing the world from someone else's perspective is vital to good communication. Without it, one is destined to get lost in his own preconceived ideas. However, moving outside oneself to empathize with others is no easy task. In fact, empathy is usually the first thing to go when conflict arises. Once empathy exits, a person is left with nothing more than his own inner dialogue about the other party. Such a self-absorbed posture puts this person at risk of being unable to comprehend what another person thinks, feels, and experiences. Without empathy, creating an understanding atmosphere is impossible.

Face-saving. Face is defined as "a psychological image that can be granted and lost and fought for and presented as a gift; it is the public self-image that every member of a society wants to claim for himself or herself; it is a projected image of one's self in a relational context."[47] Employing the qualities of genuineness, non-possessive love, and empathy allows one to communicate in a way that "saves face" for the other party. Think about it, have you ever been in an embarrassing situation where you "lost face?" It didn't feel so good, did it? Who wants to be put on the spot in a way that makes them feel inadequate? Everyone has a projected, public image, so knowing how to save the face of others is a great communication tool.

The basic principle to follow here is to be careful of what you say about others in public. As related earlier, when I embarrassed my Senior Pastor by repeating our private conversation in public, I caused him to lose face. Everyone wants a secure public image, so we must be careful with how we handle the public images of others. Communicate in a way that is authentic, yet be mindful of the need for people to save face.

Reflective listening. Listening is critical to good communication, but active listening is "a special type of listening that involves paying respectful attention to the content and feelings expressed in another's communication, hearing and understanding, and then letting the other know that he or she is being heard and understood."[48] The art of reflective listening is one of the most important communication tools to dealing with conflict. Neal Katz and John Lawyer, in their book *Communication and Conflict Resolution Skills,* highlight two skills to reflective listening: attending skills and responding skills.

Attending skills address the areas of eye contact, posture, gestures, environmental setting, and interested silence. These skills are associated with what a person *does* to keep the focus on the other party. *Responding skills,* on the other hand, involve what a person *says* to the other party to keep them in focus. These skills include acknowledgement responses, reflecting content, reflecting feelings, reflecting meaning, and summarizing.[49] Attending skills are self-explanatory, but the concept of responding skills can be clarified by this example. An individual approaches a youth worker to share her concern that an activity recently provided for students was dangerous. Listening reflectively means the youth worker would say something like, "What I hear you saying is that the activity was dangerous because we allowed students to free fall from 50 feet in the air, is that correct?" The youth worker allows the person to either affirm or restate what he meant. This approach enables the other party to feel they are being heard and will likely help keep conflict from spiraling out of control.

Assertive skills. Bolton develops the idea of assertiveness in communication. In conflict, when the fault is ours, we need to listen well. However, when someone has angered or frustrated us, we need to confront them. Here, assertive skills are in order. Assertiveness in communication is being neither a doormat nor a bulldozer, but rather a balanced approach to confronting someone. According to Bolton, the best assertive approach is a three-part message that clearly communicates your position. The message is not derogatory or demeaning, but it allows you to appropriately express your frustration. "When you throw pizza around the youth room, I get frustrated because it means more work for me." This statement employs Bolton's three elements. First, it addresses the behavior as unacceptable. Second, it expresses feelings appropriately. Finally, it addresses the effects of the behavior.[50] Obviously, assertive messages work best when they are said in a proper tone and with a controlled attitude.

In summary, communication is an important dimension to responding properly to conflict. Poor communication is avoided by laying a good foundation for healthy communication through embracing genuineness, non-possessive love, and empathy. Face-saving is vital to communicating well because it demonstrates respect for others. The skills of reflective listening and assertive messages are also great tools in responding to conflict appropriately and effectively.

resolving conflict

Having recognized what conflict is and addressed how to properly respond to it, the final step is to tackle the issue of resolving conflict. The biblical and practical dimensions of conflict resolution that are important for inside out youth workers include conflict resolution processes, forgiveness, Matthew 18:15-17, and reconciliation.

conflict resolution processes

Conflict resolution processes are strategies we can employ to resolve disagreement. Resolution takes time, effort, energy, prayer, empathy, concern, and involvement. Dudley Weeks discusses five ineffective ways of resolving conflict:

1. The Conquest Approach
2. The Avoidance Approach
3. The Bargaining Approach
4. The Quick-Fixer or Band-Aid Approach
5. The Role-Player Approach.[51]

As is evident from their names, these methods do not provide adequate resolution. Instead of using the above techniques, Weeks proposes a strategy for resolving conflict that incorporates the following nine steps:

1. Create an effective atmosphere;
2. Clarify perceptions;
3. Focus on individual and shared needs;
4. Build shared positive power;
5. Look to the future;
6. Learn from the past;
7. Generate options;
8. Develop 'doables'—the stepping-stones to action, and
9. Make mutual-benefit agreements.[52]

Each step builds on the previous one for a heightened engagement between conflicted parties, and when taken together, the steps provide a framework for the difficult task of resolution.

Similarly, Katz and Lawyer propose a seven-step strategy to solve problems. Their steps are:

1. Define the problem;
2. Identify all possible options for a solution and clarify any options that may be ambiguous;
3. Evaluate every option generated;
4. Decide on an acceptable solution;
5. Develop an implementation plan;
6. Develop a process for evaluating results, and
7. Continually talk about the experience.[53]

Both strategies have value and insights, but both are based essentially on common-sense and reason. In many conflicts, common-sense and reason will resolve disputes, but when deeply held beliefs come into play as is the case in many church conflicts, common-sense and reason are not enough. In ministry situations, it is imperative to realize the utter dependence Christians have on the Holy Spirit. He is the only one who can work on people's hearts. Without recognizing this truth, people are hard pressed to find the right perspective in the midst of more difficult conflicts. Experiencing such inadequacy is good because only by coming face-to-face with helplessness are Christians able to see God working in and through their weaknesses to accomplish His glory.

forgiveness

Thomas Baskin and Robert Enright define forgiveness as "the willful giving up of resentment in the face of another's (or others') considerable injustice and responding with beneficence to the offender even though that offender has no right to the forgiver's moral goodness."[54] They go on to point out that "forgiveness is a process, with the defining-moment decision embedded in it."[55]

Individuals process forgiveness differently. Some process offenses quickly, while others need more time to arrive at a willingness to forgive. Whatever your particular speed, be careful not to judge someone who processes differently from you. We are commanded, "Forgive one another, just as God through Christ has forgiven you" (Ephesians 4:32). The bottom line is to arrive at forgiveness; the amount of time it takes is a secondary issue.

It is also important to distinguish between forgiveness and reconciliation. "Forgiveness is intrapersonal, whereas reconciliation is interpersonal. Forgiveness is granted, whereas reconciliation is achieved."[56] The subject of reconciliation will be considered later in this chapter. For now, it's important to realize that forgiveness is something *extended to others*. It is a gift. Even if the other party does not respond favorably to forgiveness, forgiveness should not be affected by the amount of receptivity or lack thereof. In other words, forgiveness should be extended whether or not it is accepted. For example, a daughter who was abused by a father decades earlier may not be able to forgive her father until his funeral. Her forgiveness is no less real because he is unable to receive it.

Everett Worthington describes a five-step process for forgiving someone.[57] The first step, which can be as painful as it is necessary, is to *recall the hurt*. Worthington recommends praying before recalling hurt. Additionally, since past hurt can be so overwhelming, a trusted accountability partner is also recommended. Second, *empathize*. Remember the definition of *empathizing*? It's getting into the skin of the other person. Why did they hurt you? What was going on in their life that made them respond in such a way? Empathizing is trying to see life through their eyes, no matter how difficult that might be. The third step is giving *the gift of forgiveness*. In the spirit of true altruism—"unselfish regard for another person"[58]— forgiveness is a giving act that requires active participation. In fact, Worthington suggests public forgiveness because of people's potential to doubt the finality of forgiveness. By asking for forgiveness publicly, accountability for follow-through is added. The last step is no less critical: *hold on to forgiveness*. Worthington gives several suggestions for holding on to forgiveness. For example, when the pain of the event revisits a person, he needs to realize it is not necessarily due to unforgiveness. Also, Wellington challenges readers not to dwell on hurtful emotions, but to instead, remember that they have forgiven the person and get family or friends to remind them of their commitment to forgiveness.

Finally Jacqueline Mickley and Kathleen Cowles note that the "general benefits of forgiveness are thought to include psychological and spiritual growth; reduction of negative emotions such as sadness, anger, or anxiety; ability to let go of the past and get on with life; cessation of hurtful behaviors; increase in ability to reestablish or build new relationships; and transcendence."[59] Their message: forgiveness is good!

matthew 18:15-17

This passage gives clear directions for dealing with offenses caused by other Christ-followers. The goal is simple and direct—reconciliation. Although following it is not necessarily easy, it is definitely the best and most beneficial approach to reconciliation.

> **outward action**
>
> Read through Matthew 18:15-17 several times. Write down your observations. Ask yourself, "How can I live this passage and help students live this passage?"

reconciliation

Speaking of reconciliation... "Reconciliation is restoring trust in a relationship in which trust has been damaged."[60] It requires all parties to be involved, and Worthington highlights a four-step process designed to help bring about reconciliation:

1. The need to decide whether or not one is going to attempt reconciliation;
2. The need to discuss reconciliation with the other party, and
3. The need to detoxify the relationship and environment, ridding oneself of the mental and emotional baggage that hinders legitimate reconciliation. This process does not require a person to forget anything, but it does require him to stop holding on to things that impede reconciliation.

4. The need to be devoted to reconciliation. Situations will arise to test a person's resolve, but he needs to remind himself that reconciling with the other party is in the best interests of both.[61]

houston, we have a solution!

Although conflict is inevitable, it is a dynamic that can be harnessed. We have looked at three steps to confidently dealing with conflict: recognizing it, responding to it, and resolving it. This chapter has introduced you to the pitfalls and possibilities of conflict to stimulate your mind to pursue further insights into this critical issue. As inside out youth workers, we are well-acquainted with conflict, whether it is self-created or coming from the outside. Conflict is, and will continue to be, a consistent feature of student ministry. However, if you embrace conflict and seek to be a student of it, you can be confident that you will become a more effective youth worker and a better disciple maker. As an old friend of mine told me years ago, "It's not what happens, but what you do with what happens that really makes the difference." Remember those words, and the next time you face conflict and you will be able to confidently say, "Houston, we have a solution!"

inside out questions

1. Describe a difficult conflict you have faced in youth ministry? How did you handle it? What were the outcomes?

2. Do you view conflict as healthy or unhealthy? Why?

3. Which conflict style(s) do you usually employ? Why?

    - Avoiding
    - Competing
    - Compromising
    - Accommodating
    - Collaborating

4. Why is good communication so important in resolving conflicts?

5. What does "saving face" mean and why is it so important in conflict resolution?

6. Describe "reflective listening?" Why is it so important in conflict resolution?

7. Which of the following conflict resolving skills do you think is most important and why?

    - Forgiveness
    - Reconciliation

8. How can handling conflict properly help you in making disciples of Jesus Christ among teenagers?

11
the work of TEACHING

by Chris Lankford

As teachers, we're not called to simply convey a set of truths... Instead we should communicate from the depths of our encounters with God's Spirit and his Word.

Doug Fields

How would I teach my Bible study? There I was, in my beat-up '69 VW Bug—just 20 minutes before youth group—barreling down the freeway, trying to study the lesson as I drove. I recalled seeing something like this in a grisly *"Red Asphalt"* driver's ed movie during high school. The message had something to do with driving while distracted...

The dinner rush at Taco Bell had been unbelievable. I was elbow deep in burritos and red sauce when I realized I had worked past the end of my shift. Not only was I late for youth group, but now I had no time to prepare my lesson. Even worse, I saw brake lights ahead—another typical Southern California commute.

Even though my youth pastor gave out lessons weeks in advance, I usually studied (I'm using the word "studied" loosely) the same day I taught. Lately, though, I had gotten into the habit of parking in the corner of the church parking lot a few minutes before youth group to cram. Tonight there would be no cramming; it was going to be an adventure in wingin' it.

The guys in my ninth grade small group had already arrived as I stumbled into the room. "May we help you, Chris?" I was still in my work uniform, wearing a 'Hello, I'm Chris' nametag and smelling like stale tacos. I smiled as we dove into the lesson. "Open your Bibles to Exodus . . ."

I could tell something had gone terribly wrong as I walked out of the room that night, but I couldn't quite put my finger on it. My youth pastor caught me in the hallway, "Chris, how'd your group go?" My heart sank. I sheepishly replied, "Well, I'm not sure how it happened, but I think we just had one of our best nights ever." "Great job, Chris—you're turning into a great small group leader!" I choked, "Yeah, really great."

> A thorough understanding of the Bible is better than a college education.
>
> Theodore Roosevelt
> 26th President of the United States

Sitting in the front seat of my VW, I reflected on what had just happened. I was disillusioned. I barely used the Bible, but the guys still thought it was a great night. I tried to recall what I had said but everything was already blurring. "Maybe it was the Holy Spirit," I reasoned. Then fear struck as I thought, "Or maybe it was just me."

I glanced back at the lesson I was supposed to teach—Aaron and the golden calf. Oddly enough, something in the passage (Exodus 32:1-10) struck me. The people of Israel were tired of waiting for God to reveal himself to Moses on Mount Sinai. They appealed to Aaron (the vice-President, so to speak) to make them their own god. Aaron, in a mind-boggling leadership moment, collected gold from the people and created a statue of a calf. Then, in Exodus 32:4, Aaron says an odd thing. "This is your god, O Israel, who brought you up from the land of Egypt." Why would Aaron credit the golden calf with getting them out of Egypt?

If that isn't strange enough, in the next verse, Aaron tells the people, "Tomorrow shall be a feast to the LORD." I knew enough about the

Bible at that time to know when God's name was capitalized as "LORD," it was his personal name. Why was Aaron, after just crediting the golden calf for Israel's deliverance, planning to hold a feast for the Lord? Then, right in the front seat of my VW, it dawned on me. The Israelites weren't getting rid of the Lord; they were adding another god to their belief system. In other words, instead of waiting for God to reveal himself, they took matters into their hands and did things their way. They wanted to call the shots in what to believe and how to worship, and since their faith was lacking, they didn't trust God to reveal himself in his way and according to his timetable.

A brilliant light flashed in my mind. God has chosen to reveal himself through his Word, and tonight I obscured him by allowing other things to get in the way of my lesson preparation and delivery. My guys were robbed of an opportunity to see God and instead saw me. I set myself up as a golden calf—easy to see, even admire, but not what God wanted. God wanted me to make disciples of Jesus, not devotees to Chris. So that sick feeling in my stomach . . . I'm positive it was the Holy Spirit convicting me of how I had been approaching my small group teaching. But where would I go from here?

correctly dividing the Word

That moment with God in the front seat of my VW occurred twenty years ago. Wow, just remembering it gives me chills! Since then, I have taught hundreds of Bible studies for junior high and high school students with one central idea in mind. I believe an inside out youth worker *transfers God's Word to students by showing them how God has transformed his or her life through the Word.* Did you get that? It's the *why* and *how* of teaching the Bible! Why do inside out youth workers teach the Bible? To *transfer* (pass on, convey, get across) God's Word to students. How do they accomplish this transfer? By showing students how God has *transformed* (changed, altered, renovated, reconstructed) their lives through his Word.

I'll break it down a bit more. Leading Bible studies should begin and end with God's Word. In between, our lives and the lives of students should be transformed—our lives first, then students' lives. Luke 6:40 rings in my ears, "A student is not greater than the teacher. But the student who works hard will become like the teacher." This verse says we are training students to be like us—people in the process of being transformed by God and his Word. That's why I call the method of teaching I am about to describe the *life-changing, transformational approach* to teaching—the *transformational approach* for short.

> There is a book worth all other books which were ever printed.
>
> Patrick Henry
> American revolutionary leader and orator

This all sounds good, theoretically, but I can imagine what you're thinking. How can youth workers, especially volunteers, find time to develop life-changing, transformational Bible studies on a weekly basis? It's not like unlimited prep time exists. How long does this process take? My answer: a life-changing, transformational Bible study can be developed with approximately two hours of preparation. That's it! If you can carve out an extra couple of hours per week, you can be an excellent Bible teacher.

phase one: what does it say?

The first thing needed to lead a transformational study is something worthwhile to say. Conveniently, this aspect of teaching is already taken care of because God's Word is a wholly sufficient message (2 Timothy 3:16). This means the content of your talk, lesson, or study must be the Bible—plain and simple.

The question is . . . do you really teach kids God's Word?

I'll never forget a seminar I attended with my junior high students several years ago. The speaker was teaching about worship and shared how King David danced in front of the ark of the covenant (2 Samuel 6:12-15). He mentioned David danced in an ephod and said, "Isn't that cool? He was wearing an ephod! What's an ephod? It was an awesome looking hat that fit like a big sombrero. So there was David, dancing around in front of everyone with a sombrero." I could have been knocked over with a feather! I quickly glanced at my kids; they were enraptured, totally oblivious to the fact that a sombrero and an ephod are two very different pieces of clothing. They continued listening as though Jesus himself was teaching.

I pulled the leader aside after he finished speaking and the last kid was out of the room to ask him about the ephod/sombrero thing. He indicated he actually didn't know what an ephod was and just assumed it was a big hat. I explained an ephod was a tank-top/shorts underwear outfit that probably emphasized and/or revealed David's gender, which is why his wife angrily accused him of inappropriate behavior in front of ladies. I added that the point of the passage was David didn't care who saw him because he was worshipping God in the purest sense.

> *Ignorance of Scripture is ignorance of Christ.*
>
> Saint Jerome
> Catholic church father

The speaker stood there and stared at me. "Really? Wow . . . that makes a lot more sense."

Now let's face it, getting an ephod mixed up with a sombrero is ultimately no big deal. Additionally, the speaker's point regarding worship still came through, and although he didn't actually teach what was in the Bible, he did get the basic principle right. My question is what happens when students are taught something that isn't quite accurate? What happens years from now when students discover a "truth" is less than true? It destroys credibility, damages trust, and produces unnecessary questions. When handling the Word of God in order to make disciples of Jesus Christ, shouldn't we go the extra mile to know what it says? Shouldn't we teach Scripture instead of proof-texting our thoughts with Scripture? Wondering how to do this? Try the following steps.

step one: begin at least a week in advance

It is very important to begin preparation at least one week before leading a Bible study. This means if your small group meets on Tuesday evenings, your preparation should start no later than Wednesday the week before. Why? Because preparing a life-changing, transformational study is more like cooking in a crock-pot than a microwave. Slow-cooking makes for better spiritual food, and you'll understand why as the process unfolds.

> **outward action**
>
> Prayer should permeate the entire preparation process. Since this chapter primarily focuses on the skills needed to correctly divide the Word, prayer is mentioned only occasionally. However, do not mistake limited references for lack of importance. Saturate preparation in prayer!

step two: pick a passage

When teaching a lesson or small group, always begin with a passage of Scripture. If your youth pastor gives you curriculum to utilize, find out what verses the lesson is based on. *This is ALWAYS where we MUST begin.* If we start anywhere other than the Word of God, the message ultimately gets tainted or garbled. There is no inspired curriculum, only Scripture is God-breathed and able to transform (2 Timothy 3:16).

step three: look at the context

Once a passage is determined, look closely at its context. Here is a method that works well for me. You need a Bible, notepad, and curriculum (if you are using one). Start by reading the passage(s) three or four times. Write down every significant thought in the passage, followed by a question that forces clarification. For example, Ephesians 4:29 (NIV) says, "Do not let any unwholesome talk come out of your mouths, but only what is helpful for building others up according to their needs, that it may benefit those who listen." If I was leading a study on this verse, I would note these things:

1) "Unwholesome talk" is prohibited . . . what qualifies as unwholesome?
2) "helpful for building up" . . . how does this compare to unwholesome talk?

3) "according to their needs" . . . what needs is Paul talking about?

4) "that it may benefit those who listen" . . . what is the result or benefit?

step four: record your thoughts

At this point, I usually write down my own answers to these questions. Although the goal is to figure out the content of the text, I still need to identify what I think. What the text says and what I think it says will hopefully be the same, especially if I'm in tune with the Holy Spirit's guidance. However, my opinions might be wrong. Either way, it's good to get my thoughts down on paper before using any study tools.

step five: use good study tools

Now it's time for study tools. I recommend an easy-to-read commentary. A commentary is a book written by a Bible expert who has carefully studied a particular passage and has written his notes for others to study. Good commentary writers study the culture, language, and customs of the original audience to determine the original intent of a Bible author. There is a wide spectrum of commentaries available. Most youth pastors have at least one set of commentaries in their office. Be nice and perhaps you can borrow a book or two.

If you don't have a youth pastor at your church or if you, as a lay person, are the youth leader, don't worry. Your senior pastor probably has a few commentaries on every book of the Bible. Ask him for his opinion on the best commentary for the passage you are studying. Senior pastors are usually eggheads about this kind of stuff and will be delighted to help (I can say this because after years in youth ministry, I am now a lead pastor).

On another note, sometimes I am asked, "If I were to purchase a one or two volume commentary on the whole Bible, what should I buy?" Great question! I would recommend purchasing *The Bible Knowledge Commentary: Old & New Testament* by John Walvoord and Roy Zuck. It's a solid two-volume set that's easy to read and understand. Your youth pastor or lead pastor can give you other great recommendations, too.

Finally, the Internet is loaded with a wealth of commentary resources. One warning—be sure the material you use comes from a trusted source. Resources are not created equal and this has never been truer than when you evaluate resources on the Internet. There are some whacked ideas floating around cyberspace. As an FYI, resources found at *www.BibleGateway.com* are excellent; I recommend them without reservation.

The whole idea behind this kind of study is to look at what the experts have discovered through years of study and research. Their insights into ancient culture, customs, and language will help you gain an understanding of what a passage meant to the original audience. Going back to Ephesians 4:29, commentaries helped me discover that:

1) "Unwholesome talk" is "rotten" and "decaying" talk. This phrase is contrasted against "building up," which means it carries a "deconstructive" meaning. Thus, unwholesome talk is made of words that "tear down" another person.
2) "helpful for building up" relates to words that are "good, edifying, and reconstruct."
3) "according to their needs" means the words used are "just the right word at just the right moment." They are first aid for the soul.
4) "that it may benefit those who listen" means to extend God's grace to the listener.

step six: get everything together

After using study tools, go back to your original questions and answers. Compare your ideas with the ideas shared in the commentaries. Combine everything together, get rid of what doesn't fit with the text, and you're on your way to developing an excellent idea of the actual content of the Bible passage.

step seven: construct a *main idea* sentence

Can you state the major idea of the passage in a single sentence? This is the finishing step of Phase One and the most important step.

The ability to articulate the main idea of a passage in a single sentence allows you to stay focused during preparation. It can also be used to drill home the main idea over and over to students during the actual Bible lesson. Take Ephesians 4:29 for example. My sentence would read something like: "God calls us to stop using words that tear others down and instead, use words that build others up and direct people toward Jesus." Pretty cool, huh?

Even cooler, this sentence often leads to a specific outline. The above sentence could lead to a rough draft outline that might look something like this:

Main Idea: God calls us to stop using words that tear others down and instead, use words that build others up and direct people toward Jesus.

Point 1: The anatomy of words.
- What are the characteristics of "tearing down" words (what do they look like, feel like, etc.)?
- What are the characteristics of "building up" words (what do they look like, feel like, etc.)?

Point 2: Looking more in-depth at "building up" words.
- Why does Jesus want us to use these words vs. "tearing down" words?
- What constitutes "reconstructive" words?
- What constitutes words that direct people to Jesus?

Point 3: Making it practical.
- What would our group look like if we lived this truth?
- Why is this truth so difficult to live?
- How can we practically live out this truth?

wrapping up phase one

When starting Phase One, I had a Bible verse and some random ideas. Now I have something worthwhile to say straight from God's Word. All and all, I'm on the right track.

You've probably noticed the first phase is rather technical. That's okay.

Following this procedure assures we are true to the Word of God. As already stated, the Bible was written long ago in a language different from ours in a culture dissimilar to ours. Phase One helps us better understand the context and cultural distinctives surrounding particular passages and protects us from projecting personal, but incorrect, meanings on a passage.

Once you have walked through these steps a few times and grown accustomed to using particular resources, this first phase takes about an hour. The next two phases are much quicker, but don't let that tempt you into skipping this phase. Phase One forms the foundation of your entire lesson. Without it, you won't understand the context of a passage and will be in danger of teaching something other than the counsel of God.

phase two: how will it transform me?

Once we know what a passage says, we need to ask why it is important. While the first phase is technical, this one is largely personal. Why did God use these particular words? Why are they important? How do they apply to my real world?

Okay . . . it's confession time. One difficulty I have in spending personal time with the Lord is my inclination to dwell on how to transfer what I am learning to someone else. I often don't even consider what God is saying to me, all I think about is how I can teach others. But that's not the point of personal study; I am the point! God wants to transform me first before I attempt to join him in transforming others. As an inside out youth worker, I am supposed to be a living example of what it means to be transformed by His Word. If the Word of God is not transforming me, chances are it is not transforming my students. Think about it; if my small group is struggling with being kind to each other, I can guilt them with Bible verses about compassion, but verses alone are not likely to make a dent if I'm

> I am busily engaged in the study of the Bible. I believe it is God's Word because it finds me where I am at.
>
> Abraham Lincoln
> 16th President of the United States

not compassionate. However, if I teach God's Word *and* live compassionately, chances are good that they'll get it. If God is to transform students through biblical truth, he will likely transform their leaders first. Followers, by definition, follow leaders. This means that if you are to effectively teach God's Word . . . *GET TRANSFORMED!* That's what Phase Two is all about. Once we know what a text says, we have to determine its significance to us. We must make it personal. Avoid thinking about how it relates to students until you recognize how it applies to you.

step one: personalize the *main idea* sentence

How is this accomplished? The first question I ask myself is how the main idea statement from Phase One is important to me. Does anything need to change in my life for this sentence to be true? How can I personalize the sentence? In most instances, I rewrite a personalized version of the main idea statement. For instance, a personalized main idea statement from Ephesians 4:29 for me might read: "God is calling on me to stop tearing down my family and my friends with sarcastic and aggressive words and instead build them up with positive and supportive words, so I might respond well to them and make sure my words draw them closer to Christ." As you can see, I added specific difficulties (sarcasm and aggressiveness) with which I struggle. I also focused on two groups (family and friends) which are important to me. I could be even more focused by including names. You get the point.

Putting your thoughts down on paper might only take 15-20 minutes, but this phase also requires a great deal of prayer. This is one of the important reasons for

> **outward action**
>
> If you use curriculum, a main idea statement will likely be developed for you. However, don't skip personalizing the main idea. If you do, chances are you won't end up teaching from a transformed life.
>
> Also, when it's time to "pause and pray," don't hit the pause button until after reading through the curriculum. Sometimes it contains ideas that require significant planning. You should think through these ideas before taking a pause to ensure you don't run out of time later.

starting preparation a week ahead of when you teach. You need time to process what God wants to do within you.

step two: pause and pray

Once we determine what the text says and what God is specifically saying to us, wisdom says we should take time to pray. The Holy Spirit wants us to embody our personalized statement, and this process won't be instantaneous (remember the crock-pot analogy). Suspending study enables us to stop focusing on what we will teach and permits God's Word to seep into the cracks and crevices of our lives.

My suggestion? Set all of your preparation aside for three or four days. Additionally, write out your personalized main idea statement on a post-it note and stick it on the bathroom mirror or somewhere else where you'll see it everyday. Proactively participate in God's transformation of you by giving him time and space.

special considerations

Since we're pausing, let's look at two other important issues before moving to the final phase.

quiet time vs. study time

As already mentioned, I struggle with transferring everything I learn to teaching without processing it for myself. One way I minimize this weakness is by working ahead. For me, when there is little immediate urgency to transfer information, personal transformation is much more likely.

I also have learned that it is okay to allow study time for youth ministry to be a part of my personal Bible study time. I can't remember where or when I heard that this was a no-no, but I have felt guilty in the past for combining the two. For some reason, I thought my quiet times and my teaching study times needed to come from different sections of the Bible. Combining the two was completely unacceptable.

Rubbish!

I believe so strongly in the transformational effects of the process I am writing about that I am now more given to what this process does in me than any other kind of personal study. For instance, during the past couple of years, God has been doing substantial renovations at my core through a personal study in the book of John. This has also been the primary book from which I have been teaching. Since God is morphing me through this book, it only makes sense that it is what I am teaching others. I know it is popular to say, "Make sure you're studying something for your own personal growth and edification other than what you are teaching," but I couldn't disagree more! Whatever you teach, you should be transformed by it first. You will grow, and as a result, your teaching will be more authentic and powerful. Being before doing—transformation before teaching!

rifles vs. shotguns

The church I grew up in placed high value on memorizing Scripture. For instance, one school year, I memorized over 100 verses to pay for half of summer camp. Quite an incentive! This value also extended into the teaching ministry of the church. For every issue, there was a corresponding verse to apply. Struggling with swearing? Check out James 3:6-8. Premarital sex? Try Hebrews 13:4. Lust? Matthew 5:28. Gossip? Proverbs 14:23. Anger? Ephesians 4:26. Hatred? I John 4:7-8. It's as if the church had a Bible "bullet" for every problem; just pull out your rifle and take aim.

But is that how the Bible was written or how life is lived? Is it how Jesus Christ taught or how people learn? The fact is that the Bible was written as a series of narratives. Not every section of the Bible is story, but every part serves in the overall story of God. From beginning to end, the Bible has a story to tell, with Jesus Christ as the "scarlet thread" weaving through the entire narrative. The story of God, found in Scripture, is an incredible adventure revealing the glory of the Almighty.

Our lives are lived as stories as well. In fact, we simultaneously live several different "story-lines" woven together. The Bible even says that every individual narrative will ultimately bring glory to God because every knee will bow and every tongue will confess that Jesus Christ is Lord! The glory of God will be revealed in your story and in mine too.

Now here's the key. The stories of the Bible were written to teach us about how God is "overwriting" His story onto our own stories. Our lives are to tell the world about the glory of God. We are like a series of narratives the world reads. If this is truth, and I believe it is, what would it be like if our approach to teaching the Bible was like a "shotgun" rather than a "rifle?" Rifles shoot one bullet in a straight pattern, while shotguns spray pellets over a wide area. What if we taught the Bible less like a bunch of random verses that apply to varied but precise life situations and more like a series of stories with broad and varied applications? D.A. Carson, professor at Trinity International University, comments specifically on this issue as it relates to John's Gospel:

> *The precise meaning of, say, John 3:5 cannot properly be abstracted (removed) from the meaning of John 3:1-21; the meaning of John 2:4 cannot properly be sorted out without thinking through the meaning of John 2:1-11. Of course, the converse must also be said: the meaning of John 3:1-21 turns on John 3:5 (and a lot of other things as well). And the meaning of the pericope (as an individual unit within a Gospel is called) John 2:1-11 also depends on its place within the Gospel as a whole, i.e. what comes immediately before it and after it, the flow of the text and surrounding context, the place of the individual pericope within the entire Gospel.*[62]

This makes sense! When teaching students about moral purity, teach the story of David and Bathsheba and really break the text down. Help students get a sense for the heaviness of the situation. What was Uriah thinking when David got him drunk and told him to go home and sleep with his wife? What was Bathsheba doing while David plotted Uriah's death? Did either person really love the other? What was it like for David and Bathsheba to lose their baby? What kind of a God would take a baby away because of a mistake made by the parents?

This is not to say that using a rifle approach ("text-to-text" approach) is never good. Sometimes such an approach cuts right to the heart of a situation. Jesus even used this approach—especially when debating the Pharisees. But the broader and messier shotgun method ("contextual" approach) looks a lot more like real life. It's not always pretty, but we aren't either. We learn from stories because we live life as a series of intersecting stories. To throw a verse at a situation might help for a moment, but when Satan is attacking from every side, people need stories that engage life from every angle. The story of God intersecting our own stories—this is usually the best approach in teaching.

phase three: teaching to transform

To summarize . . . we have completed our study of Scripture (Phase One) and have allowed God to transform us personally by stopping to pause and pray (Phase Two). Now it's time for the final phase—teaching to transform from a transformed life.

A couple of days before leading a lesson, I sit down with my pad and paper to write out the things I have seen happening in my life. I note any personal transformation which is occurring and how the verses I've studied have been fleshed out in my life. I don't view this as some sort of magical formula; but for some reason, writing things down tends to "gel" my thoughts together and reveals applications and/or "action steps" I can use with students.

> I believe that the existence of the Bible is the greatest benefit to the human race. Any attempt to belittle it, I believe, is a crime against humanity.
>
> Immanuel Kant
> German philosopher

Notice that the focus has moved from you to your students. What's happening in their lives? What are their issues? Contextualize what you have learned in a way that a 15-year-old can grasp. Ask yourself, "How can I transfer this information in a way that will help transform my students into disciples of Jesus?" You might create a role-play situation to convey how God wants to transform your group. You could use an inspiring personal story or watch a short video that illustrates the major theme. Be creative, be interactive, be experiential, but most of all, allow God's Word to be the central message and boldly call students to transformation. If teens are given the opportunity to discover God's Word and its transforming power, as well as given an opportunity to see the truth being lived out by their inside out youth leader, then you have done your job well.

This last phase usually takes around 30-45 minutes, especially if you are using curriculum because a number of ideas have already been laid out in the curriculum. Even if you are not using curriculum, you will likely fly through this phase because of the foundation you have laid. Additionally, if you have allowed God to transform you by stopping to pause and pray (Phase Two), God has likely given you illustration ideas throughout the week (keep a notepad or your PDA handy to record these ideas). I have found that when I follow through with all three phases, the teaching preparation comes together rather quickly.

no more parking lot preparation

There you have it. That's how to prepare a life-changing, transformational Bible study in approximately two hours. The Holy Spirit can use this preparation to transform you and your students into better disciples of Jesus Christ. No more parking lot preparation. No more adventures in wingin' it. Just transferring God's Word to students by showing them how his Word has transformed you from the inside out!

inside out questions

1. Do you believe you can prepare a life-changing, transformational lesson in approximately two hours of study? Why or why not?

2. Why is it so important to start preparing for a lesson at least one week in advance?

3. How would writing out a "main idea sentence" help in teaching a Bible lesson?

4. Explain the "Phase Two: How Will It Transform Me?" process. Why is this so crucial for teaching teenagers?

5. How can God use the "pause and pray" time to help you be better prepared for teaching the Bible?

6. Do you agree with using your "quiet time" as "study time?" Why or why not?

7. What role does the life-changing, transformational approach to teaching the Bible play in making disciples of Jesus Christ among teenagers?

12

the work of PROGRAMMING

by Mike Harder

Many leaders believe they have to entertain their group to have a successful program. Wrong! Young people must experience the work of Christ if they are to grow in their faith.

Jim Burns

The sun gleams through the window at Monk's Café as Sam sits staring at his Wednesday night game plan for youth group. The topic, ironically, is Margins—Balancing Relationships in Your Life. He ponders his own juggling act as his mind wanders from youth group planning to the busy day ahead. There's no wiggle room in his schedule . . .

Wednesday, April 27, 2006

7:00AM	Preparing for "Alive" youth group meeting – Monk's Café
7:30AM	Johnson's Industries presentation – CFO & CEO – Monk's Café
8:45AM	Golf Pro Inc sales proposal – Owner – Panera Bread
10:00AM	Budget meeting – Office Boardroom
11:00AM	Revise proposals

1:00PM	*Progress report – finishing touches*	
2:00PM	*Progress report presentation – Office Boardroom*	
2:30PM	*Paper work & phone calls*	
4:00PM	*Online meeting with grad class*	
5:30PM	*Sara's soccer team practice*	
6:30PM	*Pick up refreshments for youth group*	
6:50PM	*Arrive, set-up, and greet teens as they arrive at youth group*	
7:00PM	*"Alive" – youth group meeting*	
9:00PM	*Retreat planning meeting*	
10:30PM	*Study for mid-term*	

An unsettling thought arises: he forgot the soccer bag for his 8-year-old daughter's practice. Hopefully his wife can bring it by the field and save him the extra 20 minute drive. Either way, time will be tight. Everything is tagged by the minute. No margins.

Sam sighs as his thoughts return to planning. "What can we do tonight that will be creative and fresh?" Recently, Wednesday night youth group—ironically called *Alive*—has been anything but lively. *Rut* might be a more accurate name. Every week, it's the same old thing.

- 7:00 PM – Snack / hanging out
- 7:15 PM – Game (usually pretty lame—only half the group participates)
- 7:30 PM – Announcements
- 7:35 PM – Worship songs (Sam wonders if any real worship takes place)
- 7:50 PM – Lesson
- 8:15 PM – Small group discussion and prayer (little of either actually occur)
- 8:30 PM – Hang Out (a few teens stay around, but most jet)

Sam loved youth ministry when he first got involved. And later, when asked to lead the entire group, he felt like he found his niche. Ideas for improving the youth group had been floating around in his head for some time, and this was his chance to implement those ideas. Unfortunately, most dreams hadn't materialized. There just wasn't enough "margin" (there's that word again) in his life for youth group. He wanted to give it more time and energy, but he estimated it would take a minimum of ten hours a week to really make youth meetings killer. "Where am I going to find ten extra hours?" thought Sam.

Ever feel like Sam? Ever feel like "rut" describes your weekly youth meeting or that you need a minimum of ten hours a week to develop a killer program? Wondering what you can do to make your programming creative and fresh? What if you could develop effective, meaningful programming in just a few hours a week? Would that interest you?

L.I.F.E. programming

You might be wondering why the last chapter of this book is about programming even though Kent wrote in the introduction that this book doesn't "focus on programs, processes, systems, or structures," but on "you—the youth worker." The reason we included a chapter on programming is precisely because this book is about you. If you are committed to the ArtWork of making disciples among teenagers, a chapter that speaks to the *environment* you create in your programming is totally in order. This chapter, therefore, doesn't speak to what kind of programs you should implement, but concentrates on the kind of atmosphere you should attempt to create within programming.

Also, this chapter is different from the one you just read concerning lesson preparation. The previous chapter focused on how to develop the substance of what you teach to students; this chapter is about enhancing the atmosphere within your program so that students are more likely to embrace what is being taught. Understand the difference? The last chapter was about content. This chapter is about environment.

With these clarifications in mind, there are a few assumptions I am making right from the start to keep things simple.

Assumption 1: Your youth ministry has a weekly, bi-weekly, or monthly gathering. In many parts of the country, this gathering is referred to as "youth group" and typically takes place midweek (i.e. Wednesday evenings) or on Sunday evenings. The night usually includes some of the following elements: food, games, worship music, announcements, Bible study, discussion, and prayer.

Assumption 2: The primary purpose of this regular gathering is to encourage teenagers to *grow* in their relationships with Christ and one another. This is what I will be referring to in this chapter as *growth-level programming*.

Assumption 3: Because the primary purpose of this gathering is to help teenagers grow, we will assume that most students attending fit into one of the following broad categories: 1) a follower of Christ who is also committed to your local church; 2) a teen who is somehow connected to the church (i.e. parents attend), but not necessarily highly committed to Christ or the church; 3) a friend of an attending teenager. Remember, these are *broad* categories. This does not mean visitors never attend or all students attending are Christians; rather, it is a recognition that most student who attend fit into one of these general groupings.

Assumption 4: You have a strong desire to reach lost students for Christ and to equip earnest students to reach out to peers. However, when taking into account the regular attendees, you realize that using this meeting for the purposes of outreach or ministry training is probably not best. You are not opposed to outreach or training events, but believe these gatherings should primarily be used to help believers grow.

Assumption 5: You understand this chapter is not a comprehensive look at growth-level programming, but is dedicated to helping you learn a system, which I call *L.I.F.E Programming*, that consistently enables inside out youth workers to implement practical, meaningful, and relevant ideas during a growth-level program.

L.I.F.E. elements

Now that we've spelled out the assumptions, let's move to what elements make for good L.I.F.E. programming. In the book of Acts, Luke describes a ministry that experienced God's blessing by saying:

> *They joined with the other believers and devoted themselves to the apostles' teaching and fellowship, sharing in the Lord's Supper and in prayer. A deep sense of awe came over them all, and the apostles performed many miraculous signs and wonders. And all the believers met together constantly and shared everything they had. They sold their possessions and shared the proceeds with those in need (Acts 2:42-45).*

Wow! How'd you like to lead an Acts 2 youth ministry? As an inside out youth worker who is committed to making disciples among teenagers, you can! While God cannot be manipulated, there are certain spiritual elements that, when combined together, help create an atmosphere of anticipation where seeing God stuff happen becomes a real hope. The elements are the same as the ones lived out by the early Church in Acts 2 and can be represented by the acrostic L.I.F.E.

- Life change through God's Word
- Involvement in ministry
- Fellowship with other disciples
- Exaltation of God

element one: life change through God's Word

> *They joined with other believers and devoted themselves to the apostles' teachings . . . (Acts 2:42).*

Although Jesus spent lots of time teaching the crowds, he gave significantly more time to teaching his band of followers. Why? He wanted to make sure his most committed followers understood that his teaching wasn't about facts alone, but about follow-through. According to Jesus, life change only happens within the context of obedience. This means hearing alone doesn't change anyone, *hearing* and *obeying* is what results in transformation (James 1:22-25). It's a combo deal!

In the previous chapter, Chris shared his approach to the work of teaching, so we won't concentrate on how to teach the Bible here. Our focus, instead, is on the combo deal—how to create an environment that encourages *hearing* and *obeying* God's Word in growth-level programming.

hearing God's Word . . .

Creating a listening environment in today's youth culture isn't easy. In fact, programming elements that worked just a few years ago simply don't do the trick in our media-saturated world. Most teens' lives are filled with computers, the Internet, blogs, iPods, MP3s, PS2s, cell phones, and text messages—all operating simultaneously. It is not uncommon for my 14-year-old son to be typing a research paper while carrying on three or four conversations in instant messenger. Add listening to tunes on an iPod with a TV playing in the background, and you're closer to what's "normal" for teens today.

This new "normal" means teenagers frequently struggle focusing on a single stimulant for long periods of time. While some experts suggest adult leaders should ignore cultural influences and force teens to focus, my thought is we can only teach them to focus by first reaching them within their multi-sensory world. Will teens need focusing skills for spiritual growth? You bet! But before teaching advance skills, let's help them hear God's Word within their "normal" surroundings.

How do we do this within growth-level programming? Try these tips:

Less is more! Don't try to cover too much. It's far better for teens to walk away with a solid understanding of one principle and know how to live it out than with tons of biblical data. The goal of teaching is life change, not informational download.

Mix it up. The only bad teaching method is one you always use. Most teachers have a favorite style (lecture, story telling, discussion, role playing, etc.); yet no matter how successful your style, overuse renders it ineffective.

Connect to their world. Reinforce teaching with elements from their world. Use music videos, movie clips, and PS2 games.

Surprise 'em! Teach in different locations, use guest speakers, do live interviews, have panel discussions, or videotape part of the lesson from a different location.

> ### outward action
>
> *GROUP Magazine Live,* a one-day training event hosted by Group Publishing®, is loaded with hands-on, interactive ideas. Here are two it recently promoted:
>
> **Jesus did / Jesus didn't list.** Pick a chapter in the Gospels and have teens read it and list the things Jesus did under a column entitled *Jesus Did*. Next, have them list the opposite of each action in a column entitled *Jesus Didn't*. For instance, if they write "Jesus confronted false teachers with truth" under the *Jesus Did* column; they could write "Jesus didn't embrace pluralism" under the *Jesus Didn't* column. Obviously, the more this activity is done, the larger the list grows and the better students *see and hear* the real Jesus. Post the list on the youth room wall as a constant reminder of the real Jesus!
>
> **Paraphrase Scripture.** Before teaching on a passage, have teens paraphrase the passage themselves. This will help them *hear* and actually devour the Word. Plus, you'll gain insight into what they clearly understand and what they need help understanding. Imagine doing a three-month study on a book of the Bible, like Colossians, and having kids paraphrase the entire book during your study. Now that's devouring Scripture!

Tap into the arts. Allow students to interact and respond to God's Word through painting, sculpting with clay, composing music, writing shorts stories, or videotaping original movies.

Be hands-on and interactive. Don't assume growth automatically happens in 30 minutes of lecture. Use object lessons, skits, role playing, Q&A sessions, and storytelling to make learning active. And by all means, get students to dive deep into the Bible! A good question to ask is, "Are students actively using their Bibles during our growth-level meetings?"

Use all five senses. How can your teaching include the senses of touch, taste, smell, sight, or hearing? You'll be surprised by some of the ideas that pop up when you begin using a "senses grid."

Remember, growth is a process. Spiritual growth isn't instantaneous or easily visible, and it's often an up-and-down process at best. This means it's vital to have students interacting with the Bible as much as possible.

Consistent, ongoing interface with Scripture exposes students to truth that transforms—no matter what mile marker they are at along the journey.

obeying God's Word . . .

Creating a relevant listening environment is important, but without championing obedience, spiritual transformation is unlikely. Look closely at the book of John, and you'll see how Jesus elevated follow-through over knowing facts.

- "You are truly my disciples if you keep obeying my teachings." (John 8:31)
- "If you love me, obey my commands." (John 14:15)
- "Those who obey my commandments are the ones who love me." (John 14:21)
- "You are my friends if you obey me." (John 15:14)

How can we follow Jesus' example and champion obedience in growth-level programming?

Equip in life skills. Don't just say God expects obedience, show students what follow-through looks like. Break it down to specific life skills and give them an opportunity in your program to practice these skills.

Focus on the other 166 hours of the week. Challenge teens to be different in attitude, conviction, and lifestyle when they *leave* youth group, and provide support tools outside the program such as web sites with ideas for applying the teaching or a blog that allows teens to respond to the lesson.

Promote heart habits. Supplement your teaching with opportunities for students to participate in spiritual disciplines like tithing, journaling, devotional reading, Bible study,

> *Religion seems very much a part of the lives of many U.S. teenagers, but for most of them it is in ways that seem quite unfocused, implicit, in the background, just part of the furniture.*
>
> Dr. Christian Smith
> associate chair of sociology at the
> University of North Carolina
> from his book *Soul Searching*

prayer, fasting, and times of solitude. Provide training, simple tools, and accountability structures to foster follow-through.

Process together. It's important to allow teens time to digest what is taught. Therefore, intertwine discussion into lessons.

Take action. Have students take immediate action! Ask them to write letters to God or participate in an appropriate act of service. Connect hearing with immediate obedience whenever possible.

Provide adult support. Connecting students with adult mentors, small group leaders, and accountability partners is perhaps the best idea for championing obedience. Student-led ministry is great, but it cannot replace the positive influence that caring adults provide. While some youth workers attempt to dispute this reality, the evidence lines up strongly against them. Study after study not only supports teenagers' need to have significant relationships with caring adults, but most even indicate that students themselves realize this need. The National Study of Youth and Religion is the most intensive study ever done on American young people and their religious faith. One of its findings was "the lives of (religious teens) are, compared to less religious teens, statistically more likely . . . to be linked to and surrounded by adults, particularly non-parent adults who know and care about them . . . (This) tends to contribute to more positive, successful outcomes in youth's lives."[63] In fact, lead researcher Dr. Christian Smith of the University of North Carolina states, "Adults inescapably exercise immense influence in the lives of teens—positive and negative, passive and active. The question, therefore, is not whether adults exert influence, but what kinds of influence they exert."[64] If you want to champion obedience, facilitate adult-teen relationships. It's the most practical step you can take to help students follow through in their commitment to Christ.

To wrap up, creating an environment in your growth-level program where God's Word can be *heard* and *obeyed* is critical if you want to make disciples among teenagers. To make sure these are realities in your ministry, continually ask yourself good questions. How can life change in students be measured? What does it look like? How can teaching be reinforced? What can we do to better equip teens to live what is taught?

element two: involvement in ministry

> *And all the believers met together constantly and shared everything they had. They sold their possessions and shared the proceeds with those in need (Acts 2:44-45).*

The second ingredient to growth-level programming is involvement in ministry. As James writes, "Faith is dead without good deeds" (2:26). This means inside out youth workers should foster a *serving others* tone by providing opportunities for teens to care for peers within the group and reach out to peers outside the group. There are four important aspects to involving others in ministry.

> *Whenever possible share Christ, if necessary use words.*
>
> St. Francis of Assisi
> 13th century Catholic priest

Ministry is about sacrificial serving. Did Acts 2:43-44 impact you? Those early believers knew how to serve! What's more, they realized their possessions didn't ultimately belong to them. This isn't the case for most North American Christians. We are extremely materialistic and most Christian youth have been spoiled to the point that they live in a "me-centered" universe. Yet Christ taught an entirely different philosophy. His attitude was: I came to serve, not be served (Mark 10:45). He served his Father which, in turn, meant he served others. He washed feet, helped friends fish, saved a wedding host from embarrassment, and cared for the sick and dying. Jesus, God in the flesh, was the exemplary servant, and the group in Acts 2 followed Jesus' example. They fought their natural lean toward self-indulgence and embraced com-

> *People don't care how much you know until they know how much you care.*
>
> Howard Hendricks
> author, Bible teacher

munity-centered living. No longer perceiving the blessings God gave them as items to enjoy alone, they looked to meet the needs of others.

What would happen if people in our youth ministries and churches no longer saw their stuff as their own, but rather as tools to bless others? Can you imagine? Our ministries would have much more impact if we learned to sacrificially serve each other and then practiced this same kindness with those outside our ministry walls.

Ministry often requires deconstruction. To successfully move teens into sacrificial serving, some mental models like the materialistic one just mentioned must be deconstructed. To deconstruct flawed mental models, don't just teach serving; use growth-level programming to initiate serving both inside and outside the church. Use service projects and weekly volunteerism to give students hands-on, practical experience in serving others.

Lifestyle is the ultimate goal in serving. Go to most average-size youth groups in America, and you'll discover they have "student ministry teams." However, probe a bit and you'll also discover these teams are primarily task-focused. The Welcoming Team. The Drama Team. The Tech Team. The Stage Crew. The Worship Band. Each team has a specific *task* to fulfill to help a program run. But is the fulfillment of tasks the ultimate goal in ministering to others? Is it the kind of ministry to which Jesus called disciples? Don't misunderstand, tasks are important and can be considered ministry. Yet, the truest form of ministry is *lifestyle*. It's about relationally reaching out to and serving others. See the difference?

Think about it this way ... spiritually lost people can run sound equipment, act in a drama, or set up a stage, but true redeeming min-

---

outward action

Consider these ideas to get teens serving...

- Serve once a month in the nursery
- Rake leaves for the elderly
- Set up a tutoring program that allows older teens to tutor younger teens
- Host free community car washes
- Sponsor "Date Nights"—free babysitting service a few times a year for young couples with kids.

istry can only be done by those who have been redeemed. The point here isn't that task teams are evil; not only are they not bad, they're necessary. However, we paint a poor picture of ministry when it's only connected to tasks. It gives the impression that a person can show up to church, do a task, and be done with ministry for the week. But ministry isn't exclusively about doing a task; it's supposed to be a way of life.

My suggestion . . . champion serving others as the highest form of ministry. Help students see that the ongoing relationships they create in reaching out and caring for others are much more significant than performing a task.

Use the ladder approach to help teens reach a lifestyle ministry. How do students develop the "eyes of a servant" to the point that they live ministry as a lifestyle? This might seem like an insurmountable task, but as with other things, each small step adds up. For instance, having teens en-

> *An individual has not started living until he can rise above the narrow confines of individualistic concerns to the broader concerns of all humanity*
>
> Martin Luther King, Jr.
> 20th century civil right champion

courage one another regularly during group meetings teaches them to value people over stuff. That's one step. Getting them involved in task-serving within your group is another step. So are service projects that reach out to people. With each small step, if you help students think about how to apply what they're learning to real life, before you know it, the Holy Spirit will enable them to step their way into a ministry lifestyle!

element three: fellowship with other disciples

> *They joined with other believers and devoted themselves to . . . fellowship, sharing in the Lord's Supper and in prayer. They . . . met in homes for the Lord's Supper and shared their meals with great joy and generosity (Acts 2:42, 46).*

A quick glance at typical teenage blogs reveals that many kids today live in a vacuum without meaningful relationships. Despite the variety of communication venues available, most teens are intensely lonely. "Just below the surface, today's mid-adolescents feel a sense of loneliness and isolation that betrays the confidence with which they present themselves, even to one another."[65] This means inside out youth workers who are committed to making disciples of Jesus Christ have a tremendous opportunity to help teens experience God's desires for healthy relationships. Think about it . . . the Church is God's answer to loneliness. We are the "family" of God, and being adopted into this family is what restores our relationship with God and with one another.

The Bible paints a vivid picture of what these restored, authentic relationships look like by using the word *koinonia* (fellowship). "Its basic idea is sharing, but it is used also to denote intimacy and fellowship . . . The nineteen occurrences of *koinonia* in the New Testament suggest that the church used this word for the unique sharing that Christians have with God and with other Christians."[66] Additionally, "true fellowship focuses on God and helps people to remember the good things he has done, which, in turn, cause praise."[67]

How do inside out youth workers develop authentic fellowship within growth-level programming? How can they encourage students to share life with one another, remember God's goodness, and in turn, praise him? Here are three suggestions . . .

> I've always been prone to episodes of extreme loneliness and longing for a place where I could feel safe enough to let down my defenses. Because I was an extremely outgoing and energetic little girl/adolescent, no one would ever guess how alone I really felt . . . just wish sometimes I could find somewhere to belong.
>
> high school student
> quoted in the book *Hurt* by Chap Clark

Focus on safety. More than anything, students need safe places, and they know it. Group Publishing® surveyed more than 10,000 teenagers, asking them to rate the factors that make them want to commit and stay committed to a youth group. Out of ten options, "A welcoming atmosphere where I can be myself" won (interestingly, "A fast-paced, high-tech, entertaining ministry approach" came in dead last). Unfortunately, most teens are more accustomed to feeling emotionally beaten up than built up. It happens in schools, extracurricular activities, and sometimes even at home. The emotional scars cause callousness and an apprehension to being real. Protective shields go up quickly and only come down (very slowly) when teens sense they will be accepted as they are—triumphs, failures, talents, and flaws. Inside out youth workers must strive to create emotional havens in their youth groups where students are freed from the fear of rejection and know their uniqueness in Christ will be celebrated. Only by creating such a culture will teens put down their shields and honestly share feelings, struggles, and aspirations (see chapter 8 for more ideas on creating a safe, loving environment).

There are numerous ways to foster this kind of culture, but one of the best is to establish a "no cuts" policy. I've done this in every ministry I've led. The official name I've given it is *7-Ups*. Here are the guidelines . . .

- No one is allowed to critique a person's physical features or say anything negative about someone's personhood.
- If someone violates the "no cuts rule," he or she has to affirm the person with seven positive comments.
- This guideline is a non-negotiable for staying involved in youth ministry (in other words, I'm willing to "lose" students, even popular ones, if they will not abide by this guideline).

This simple step, when consistently applied, has paid huge safety dividends.

Add actions. When Joe's mom died, his world collapsed; yet he experienced a haven of safety within our ministry. During his grieving, teens didn't know what to say; words of comfort just weren't coming to most of them. But they soon discovered their presence spoke more than words. As Joe grieved his loss one night, teen after teen

> *Shared joy is a double joy; shared sorrow is half a sorrow.*
>
> Swedish Proverb

ministered to him. They hugged him, cried with him, and sat in silence with him. The Holy Spirit intuitively gave each one just the right response to demonstrate God's incarnational love for Joe. I have never been more proud of a group of students!

I also have never been more proud of a group of adult volunteers! My delight wasn't in how they ministered to Joe directly, even though they were outstanding. My satisfaction came from realizing they had modeled authentic fellowship so well that students, led by the Holy Spirit, intuitively knew what to do. They knew what actions to take to care for a hurting friend.

Multilayer adults. We've already discussed the role adults should play in the lives of students. Simply stated, students need supportive adults investing in them—not only parents, but adults outside their family. Yet, here's one more bit of insight: one caring adult is probably not enough. Chap Clark, in his book *Hurt*, describes how the American culture has systematically abandoned youth: "As society in general moved from being a relatively stable and cohesive adult community intent on caring for the needs of the young to a free-for-all of independent and fragmented adults seeking their own survival, individual adolescents found themselves in a deepening hole of systemic rejection. This rejection . . . is the root of the fragmentation and calloused distancing that are the hallmarks of (today's) adolescent culture."[68] At school, in neighborhoods, and even at church, most students experience a sense of abandonment by adults. This lack of adult involvement and input, in turn, leads them to rely almost exclusively on their own judgment and the judgment of their peers to pilot the teenage journey. The problem is that neither they nor their peers have enough life experience or skill to adequately navigate all the challenges associated with the teenage years. Only caring adults can fill this role.

One of Clark's suggestions for combating this problem is to make sure each student has several adult advocates who know and care for him or her.

> *A popular myth that many of us have grown up with is the idea of a single role model . . . Unfortunately, an individual does not have the ability to be present in the variety of ways an adolescent needs . . . Research has consistently demonstrated that several positive and*

> *supportive (adult) relationships that offer the same messages must be present to have an effect on the life of a child. If a child has a mentor who is gentle, supportive, and affirming during a weekly encounter, yet the rest of the week he hears that he is lazy, stupid, and incompetent, the negative voices will win out. One fan, even a great one, is not enough.*
>
> *Every adult must attempt to add to the cumulative message of protection, nurture, warmth, and affection. It takes several, if not dozens, of consistently supportive and encouraging messages to counteract the effects of systemic abandonment. By far the best way to help our young is by being a chorus of support and a choir of commitment.*[69]

What does this mean for inside out youth workers who are trying to make disciples of Jesus Christ among teenagers? We need to keep a "chorus of support" in mind when recruiting adults. Don't just enlist volunteers for crowd control, food prep, or teaching—relationship building should be job one for volunteers! Most should commit to only one youth ministry program, then spend the rest of their time "doing life" with students. Teens need several sharp, caring adults who love them, invest in them, and shepherd them, so be sure your ministry does whatever it takes to make this a reality.

element four: exaltation of God

> *A deep sense of awe came over them all, and the apostles performed many miraculous signs and wonders . . . They worshipped together at the Temple each day, met in homes for the Lord's Supper . . . (Acts 2:42, 46).*

Ever catch your thoughts drifting during a worship service as your lips move by memory to the words of a song? I have. When it happens, I usually ask, "Was that really worship?"

What is worship? Singing to a certain style of music? What we do on Sunday mornings? Praying? While these are legitimate facets of worship, exalting God goes far beyond any one component.

Worship is the total focus of our entire being on our Savior and King and is by no means limited to a weekly gathering. Exalting God should ooze throughout every aspect of our lives, seven days a week. As Jerry Bridges writes, "God is not impressed with our worship on Sunday morning at church if we are practicing 'cruise-control' obedience the rest of the week. You may sing with reverent zest or great emotional fervor, but your worship is only as pleasing to God as the obedience that ac-

> ### inside info
>
> Ever have students regularly raise their hands during worship, even cry, yet have serious patterns of sin running through the fabric of their lives? I remember two such students. During our worship celebration, they raised hands, fell to their knees, and shed tears. When asked why, they would say, "Because we're so moved." Yet immediately after the service, they would often sleep with one another. Even more, their actions and attitude throughout the week did not come close to resembling true follower-ship.
>
> Obviously, they had a wrong view of worship. They saw it as a moving, emotional event that occurred once a week, not as a way of life. In reality, these students were worshipping the music and event more than God. True worship always includes obedience.

companies it."[70] If growth-level experiences are to help students understand true worship, here are a few things to keep in mind.

Corporate worship. Make sure students understand that worship during youth group is simply a chance to corporately (i.e. together with other believers) express to God what we should be expressing to him every day through word and deed. In other words, help students realize worship is not just an event or something they do at youth group; it's a lifestyle. As Paul exhorts, we are to "offer our bodies as living sacrifices, holy and pleasing to God—that is to be our spiritual act of worship" (Romans 12:1–NIV).

Get creative. There are tons of solid youth ministry resources geared towards helping teens see worship as more than singing songs, and most include creative motifs that connect well with this generation of students. For instance, some attempt to use all five senses to express adoration to

> *Worship is the essential and central act of the Christian.*
>
> Eugene Peterson
> author of *The Message*

Christ. This is great for corporate worship with students because many will engage more when they can see, touch, taste, feel, and hear something. In fact, a good example comes out of our ministry. For a time, we were unable to have music during youth gatherings because it was too loud for groups using rooms around us. So . . . we got creative. Worship experiences included writing out prayers of thanksgiving, prayer walks, expressing ourselves through sculpting with clay, and writing personal psalms to God. Our teens loved these out-of-the-box experiences!

Ask questions. Perhaps the best way to keep worship experiences fresh is to ask good questions:

- Is our worship God-focused?
- Can we change the environment by either changing the room or going elsewhere to focus better?
- Are our tools for worship (worship band, singing, etc.) being overused? What other elements could be incorporated?
- How can we create an E.P.I.C. environment (experiential, participatory, image-driven, and community-based)?[71]
- Can we involve all five senses?
- How do we help teens practice worship as a lifestyle?

L.I.F.E. mixture

Once youth workers understand the four elements to L.I.F.E. programming, they're ready to develop effective, creative programming in just a few hours a week. That's right, it doesn't have to take ten hours a week to keep things fresh. Here's all you need to do . . .

team approach

First, if at all possible, use a team for program planning. "Creativity is not for mavericks. What's better: a solo home run or the grand slam? Better yet, a game well-played by one person and lost or a game won? Alone, you'll fall short, period."[72] Ideas, as well as implementation, are stronger and take less time when others are involved.

think series

If you're in the habit of planning week-to-week—STOP! This is the main culprit that makes programming so difficult. Instead, plan series. Series planning allow the:

- Program team to meet once per series.
- Four L.I.F.E. ingredients to be stretched throughout the series instead of crammed into each night.

Here's how this works. Let's say your growth-level ministry meets on Wednesday nights and you have a six-week series on the Parables of Jesus coming up. Your program team could meet for breakfast to decide what parables to cover, what creative L.I.F.E. ideas to use, and who is responsible for what. Plus, if you come up with one creative idea for each L.I.F.E. ingredient, the series approach allows you to strategically decide when to use each idea instead of trying to cram all of them into one night.

> The difficulty lies not so much in developing new ideas as in escaping from old ones.
>
> John Maynard Keynes
> 20th century economist

By the way, even if this breakfast meeting takes three hours, if you average this out over the six week series, it adds up to be only thirty minutes per week. That's a pretty good use of time!

think variety

As long as you're planning a series, keep variety in mind as well. Who says every growth-level meeting has to look the same? Remember the "rut" example from earlier:

- 7:00 PM – Snack and hang out
- 7:15 PM – Game
- 7:30 PM – Announcements
- 7:35 PM – Worship
- 7:50 PM – Lesson
- 8:15 PM – Small group discussion and prayer

What if your six-week series looked more like this?

- Week 1 – All small groups hang out together at a restaurant or park (i.e. *Fellowship with Growing Believers* element). That's it, nothing else!
- Weeks 2-4 – Regular Meeting Schedule.
- Week 5 – Students participate in a ministry project as a way to respond to what has been taught over the past three weeks (i.e. *Involvement in Ministry* element).
- Week 6 – Students participate in a worship and testimony night to share what God has done in their lives through this series (i.e. *Fellowship with Growing Believers* and *Exaltation of God* elements)

Adding the right mix of variety to a series brings energy, anticipation, and even surprise to what was once considered routine and boring.

start early

When planning a series, it's always better to start a few weeks early. My suggestion would be to have your planning meeting at least one or two weeks before the start of a series.

do few things and do them well

Ever tried washing a car without the nozzle attachment? The water simply trickles out the end of the hose. Stick on the nozzle and water shoots out with great force. Doing few things well is similar to putting a nozzle on your programming! It allows you to focus your attention on the few ideas that are most likely to create a L.I.F.E. environment. This means pulling out tons of bells and whistles for each night is actually counter-productive. Instead, focus on one, or at the most, two programming ideas per night and implement them well.

Let's use our Parables of Jesus series idea again as an example. Imagine you have two good ideas for the story of the Prodigal Son—one is a video that highlights Scriptural truth (i.e. *Life Change through God's Word* element), and the other is a responsive worship experience (i.e. *Exaltation of God* element). Both items could fit into one night, but it would be tight. So how do you choose? You don't. Instead, stretch the Prodigal Son story over two weeks. During week one, show the video and dive deep into the Word. If done correctly, you'll experience both *Life Change through God's Word* and *Fellowship with Growing Believers*. During week two, show the video again as a jumping off point for your creative worship experience. You could even stretch this into a third week by creating a ministry project that revolves around this parable's truths (i.e. *Involvement in Ministry* element).

think excellence, not perfection

Want to hit the wall? Then strive for perfection. As veteran youth pastor David Chow says, "I hit the wall when I put my trust in the perfect program instead of the perfect God. It was only after giving up on having the perfect youth program that I could accept and embrace ministry for what it ultimately really was—caring for people, not just carrying out a plan."[73]

No program can be perfect, but every program can be excellent. Excellence means doing the very best you can with the resources you have. Inside out youth workers use their time, energy, budget, volunteers, facilities, and equipment to the best of their abilities when designing and developing their growth-level program, but they don't expect perfection.

things to avoid

Finally, here are a few mistakes youth workers make in trying to retool their growth-level programs. You'd be wise to avoid them.

- Don't make significant programming changes (i.e. changing meeting nights or program emphasis) until you have prayed fervently.
- Don't make such changes without doing your homework. Research your community, survey teens in your group, and find out what's been done in the past.
- Don't make changes until key players are on board (i.e. lead pastor, leadership team, volunteers, parents, etc.)
- Communicate changes to *everyone* (i.e. students, parents, board members, the janitor, etc.).

conclusion

There you have it—four L.I.F.E. elements to growth-level programming and practical guidelines for implementing them. Follow the ideas presented in this chapter, and you will be on your way to creating an environment that is conducive to students experiencing a growing relationship with Christ and others!

inside out questions

1. How can a solid growth-level program help you make disciples of Jesus Christ among teenagers?

2. Chapter 11 focused on teaching God's Word. In this chapter, the first element of L.I.F.E. programming was "Life Change through God's Word." How did this element add to what was discussed in Chapter 11?

3. What are some things you can do to create a "hearing" and "obeying" environment in your growth-level program?

4. Do you agree that "relationship" serving is a higher level of ministry than "task" serving? Why or why not?

5. What will happen long-term if teenagers never see the difference between task serving and relationship"serving?

6. Why is "multilayer-ing adults" so important in a growth-level program? What can you do to multilayer adults?

7. During corporate worship experiences, how can you help students learn the difference between worshipping God and worshipping the worship experience?

8. How can you help students live a lifestyle of worship?

9. When planning a growth-level series, why is it important to think?

   - Team
   - Series
   - Variety

inspiring true ArtWork
you get what you expect

by Kent Julian

Now glory be to God! By his mighty power at work within us, he is able to accomplish infinitely more than we would ever dare to ask or hope.

The Apostle Paul

I write these final words from my favorite coffee shop. It's my second office and the place I often meet other youth workers to chat about life and ministry. If you and I were meeting, and you had just finished reading this book, I'd ask you a couple of questions . . .

- *Do you want to be an inside out youth worker?*
- *Are you really committed to the ArtWork of making disciples among teenagers?*

Then I'd give you two words of advice . . .
START NOW!

Take action. Get moving. Start today. Don't think you have to know everything to begin, just get going and learn along the way.

Don't get me wrong, I'm a huge proponent of reading and training, but

> Men and women are limited not by the place of their birth, not by the color of their skin, but by the size of their hope.
>
> John Johnson
> founder of *Ebony* and *Jet* magazines

being an inside out youth worker takes action. You'll never be perfectly prepared to start, so the best advice I could leave with you is to just dive in. Take the plunge! Continue to learn and grow as you go, and within no time, you'll be an inside out youth worker.

I'd probably also share a few other thoughts I've come to call the *E's of Excellence* (I know, really corny, but it helps me remember) . . .

First, remember that basically every idea in this book is *environmental*. This means that both the art of being and the work of doing are designed to create space for God to work in and through you. Focus on your role and trust God to do his.

Second, speaking of trusting God, what are your *expectations* in ministry? Do you believe God is "able to accomplish infinitely more than we would ever dare to ask or hope?" (Ephesians 3:20). Are you living and leading accordingly? I have found that an attitude of expectancy that is tied to hope in God—instead of to external conditions or circumstances—is the key to being effective in youth ministry. In many ways, we get what we expect, so go ahead and live as if you really believe God can do more than what you can think or imagine. As many of the authors of this book will testify, when you do, he does!

Third, as long as you are going to have an attitude of expectancy, be sure to also do your part and *exceed expectations*. Whether you agree with popular self-help guru Wayne Dyer or not, he is definitely right about one thing . . . "It's never crowded along the extra mile." So travel the extra mile and exceed expectations. I hate saying this, but youth ministry attracts many people who use being "relational" and "authentic" as excuses for laziness. By all means, be relational and authentic, but be that way while striving for excellence.

Fourth, even though you should strive to excel, don't forget to *embrace simplicity*. The ArtWork of making disciples among teenagers is not complicated; it's simply being before doing. Therefore, if you want to be an inside out youth worker, don't make things harder than they are, just live . . . inside out. Focus on one of the being qualities or one of the doing actions described in this book every few months, and within no time, you'll see yourself becoming inside out.

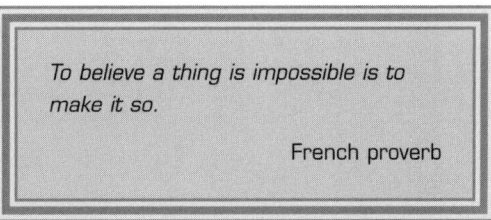

> To believe a thing is impossible is to make it so.
>
> French proverb

Finally, *earnestly lean into* the opportunities God grants you. No matter if you are serving four teenagers or four hundred, when you are available to God, he usually shows up. And God showing up—more than great resources, spectacular facilities, or dynamic programs—is what creates momentum. I have experienced this reality while serving in a megachurch context, as well as when leading just a handful of students. I have also missed this reality in both settings. Don't miss out on God doing incredible work in the midst of your ministry; be faithful at your post by earnestly leaning into every opportunity.

I hope you have enjoyed reading this book as much as we have enjoyed writing it. Our prayer is that it won't be just another resource that gets put on your shelf, but one that inspires both volunteers and full-time youth pastors to join God in making disciples of Jesus Christ among students by living inside out!

Let's have coffee again real soon.

With great respect and admiration for who you are and what you do,

Kent Julian (for the entire writing team)

notes

[1] http://www.quotationspage.com/quote/3029.html

[2] Jack Canfield, *The Success Principles* (New York; HarperCollins Publishers, 2005), 249.

[3] Lawrence O. Richards, *Expository Dictionary of Bible Words* (Grand Rapids: Zondervan, 1985), 226.

[4] http://www.dict.die.net/art

[5] http://www.biblebb.com/files/MAC/sg1670.htm

[6] Ibid.

[7] http://www.biblegateway.com/resources/commentaries/index.php?action=getCommentaryText&cid=7&s0urce=1&seq=i.55.5.8

[8] Ibid.

[9] Ibid.

[10] http://www.whm.org/pdf/Sonship%20Intro.pdf

[11] Biblical Discernment Ministries website (http://www.rapidnet.com/~jbeard/bdm/Psychology/self-est/key.htm)

[12] Billie Davis, *Self-esteem: Essential or Dangerous,* Sunday School – Learning to Live the Life website (http://sundayschool.ag.org/01Teachers/t_el_0308esteem%20.cfm)

[13] In Romans 3:10-18, Paul quotes from the following passages: Psalm 14:1-3; 53:1-3; 5:9; 140:3; 10:7; Isaiah 59:7-8; Psalm 36:1

[14] Randy Alcorn, *Self-love and Scripture*, Eternal Perspective Ministries website (http://www.epm.org/articles/psyself.html)

[15] I have seen this quote in several places, but cannot find its source.

[16] Chuck Swindoll, *Improving Your Serve* (Waco: Word, 1981).

[17] O'Reilly, "Future," *Fortune,* 24 July 2000, 146.

[18] MaryAnn Johanson, film critic, www.flickfilosopher.com, quoted in Neil Howe and William Strauss, *Millennials Rising* (New York: Vintage Books, 2000), 4.

[19] Ibid., 7.

[20] Ibid., 19.

[21] All bullet points are summaries of statements made throughout the book *Millennials Risings*.

[22] Christian Smith, *Soul Searching* (Oxford: University Press, 2005), 260, 262.

[23] Ibid., 262.

[24] Lawrence Tabak, "If Your Goal is Success, Don't Consult These Gurus" (http://pf.fastcompany.com/magazine/06/cdu.html)

[25] Stephen R. Covey, A. Roger Merrill, and Rebecca R. Merrill, *First Things First* (New York: Simon & Schuster, 1994), 75.

[26] Some manuscripts include ""prayer and fasting" in verse 29.

[27] Jim Cymbala, *Fresh Faith* (Grand Rapids: Zondervan, 1999), 45.

[28] *What Matters Most: Jesus Everyday in Every Way*, Group Magazine Live 2005-2006 Workshop booklet (Loveland, CO: Group Publishing, 2005), 19.

[29] Carl Wilson, *With Christ in the School of Disciple Building* (Fayetteville, GA: Worldwide Discipleship Association Books, 1976), 223.

[30] John Rosemond, *Teen-Proofing: Fostering Responsible Decision Making in Your Teenager*, (Kansas City: Andrews McMeel Publishing, 2001), 8.

[31] Rick Lawrence, "Are Your Kids Real-World Ready?" *Group Magazine*, January/February, 2005, 91.

[32] Michael J. Bradley, *Yes Your Teen Is Crazy: Loving Your Teen Without Losing Your Mind* (Harbor, WA: Harbor Press, 2003), 24.

[33] Steve Turner, *Imagine: A Vision for Christians in the Arts* (Downers Grove: InterVarsity, 2001), 38.

[34] Tony Alessandra and Michael J. O'Connor, *The Platinum Rule: Discover the Four Basic Business Personalities —and How They Can Lead You to Success* (New York: Warner Books, 1996).

[35] Leonard Sweet, *Post-Modern Pilgrims: First Century Passion for the 21st Century Church* (Nashville: Broadman & Holman Publishers, July, 2000), 126.

[36] http://www.preachingplus.com/DisplaySermon.aspx?id=199

[37] Resources that express the "tribe" concept include, but are not limited to, Neil Howe and Robert Strauss, *Millennials Rising* (New York: Vintage Books, 2000); Patricia Hersch, *A Tribe Apart* (New York: Ballantine Books, 1998); Chap Clark, *Hurt* (Grand Rapids: Baker Academic, 2004); and Rick Lawrence, *Trendwatch* (Loveland: Group Publishing, 2002).

[38] Doug Fields, "The Power of Affection" (*Group Magazine,* November/December 2005), 36.

[39] Don Everts, *God in the Flesh* (Colorado Springs: Intervarsity Press, 2004),

[40] Doug Fields, "The Death of Cool, The Birth of Real" (*Group Magazine*, January/February, 2006).

[41] Wayne Rice and David Veerman, *Understanding Your Teenager* (Nashville: Word Publishing, 1999), 117-119.

[42] C.R. Mitchell, *The Structure of International Conflict* (New York: St. Martin's Press, 1981), 17.

[43] William W. Wilmot & Joyce L. Hocker, *Interpersonal Conflict* (Boston: McGraw Hill), 1978.

[44] Robert Bolton, *People Skills: How to Assert Yourself, Listen to Others, and Resolve Conflicts* (New York, Simon & Schuster, 1979), 259.

[45] Ibid, 262-268.

[46] Ibid, 270.

[47] David W. Augsburger, *Conflict Mediation Across Cultures: Pathways and Patterns* (Louisville: Westminster John Knox Press, 1992), 85.

[48] Neil H. Katz & John W. Lawyer, *Communication and Conflict Resolution Skills* (Dubuque, IA: Kendall/Hunt Publishing Company, 1985), 27.

[49] Ibid, 29-30.

[50] Ibid, 143.

[51] Dudley Weeks, *The Eight Essential Steps to Conflict Resolution* (New York: Tarcher/Putnam Books, 1992), 16-30.

[52] Ibid, 71-234.

[53] Katz & Lawyer, 51-53,

[54] Thomas W. Baskin & Robert D. Enright, "Intervention Studies on Forgiveness: A Meta-Analysis" (*Journal of Counseling and Development,* 2004), 80.

[55] Ibid, 82.

[56] Everett L. Worthington & Dewitt T. Drinkard, *Promoting Reconciliation Through Psychoeducational and Therapeutic Interventions* (Journal of Marital and Family Therapy, 2000), 94.

[57] Worthington, *Forgiving and Reconciling: Bridges to Wholeness and Hope* (Downers Grove: InterVarsity Press, 2003), 78-166.

[58] Ibid, 119.

[59] Jacqueline Ruth Mickley & Kathleen Cowles, *Ameliorating the Tension: Use of Forgiveness for Healing* (ONS Foundation, 2001), 31.

[60] Worthington, *Forgiving and Reconciling: Bridges to Wholeness and Hope,* 170.

[61] Ibid.

[62] D.A. Carson, *The Gospel According To John* (Grand Rapids: Eerdmans, 1991), 101.

[63] Christian Smith, *Soul Searching* (Oxford: Oxford University Press, 2005), 227.

[64] Ibid., 28.

[65] Chap Clark, *Hurt* (Grand Rapids: Baker Academic, 2004), 144.

[66] Ajith Fernando, *The NIV Application Commentary: Acts* (Grand Rapids: Zondervan, 1998), 120.

[67] Ibid., 123.

[68] Chap Clark, *Hurt*, 33.

[69] Ibid., 183.

[70] Jerry Bridges, *The Disciplines of Grace* (Colorado Springs: NavPress, 1994).

[71] Original idea of EPIC adopted, but altered somewhat, from Leonard Sweet's writings.

[72] Jeff White, *Hoy Wow* (Loveland: Group Publishing, 2004), 31.

[73] David Chow, *The Perfect Program* (Colorado Springs: TH1NK, 2005), 20.

WANT TO BREAK THROUGH THE COMMUNICATION ROADBLOCKS WITH YOUR TEEN?

What turns your teen off and on in terms of communication? Do you find yourself talking with him or at him? What will it take to open her heart—or his mouth, for that matter?

If you love your teen but find the communication lines jumbled lately, the ideas in this book will help! Research constantly reveals: If you're a parent, you ARE the most important person in your teenager's life. And with a little help in the translation, you may find out she's been telling you that all along.

Definitely one of the best books I've ever read on communicating with teenagers.
　Wayne Rice, Co-founder of Youth Specialties

This book offers a straightforward approach to building communication skills with your teenager. It addresses one of the most challenging areas of parenting teens with simple, easy-to-follow language and ideas that will help you create an environment where communication happens naturally in your home.
　　　　　　　Doug Fields, High School Pastor, Saddleback Church

Kent and Connie give you all the tools you need to build the communication bridge.
　　　　　Barry St. Clair, President, Reach Out Youth Solutions

This book has fifty-two incredibly practical lessons on develop a better relationships with your teenager. It is practical, challenging, and affirming—a must-read for every parent!
　　　　　　　　Jim Burns, PhD, President, HomeWord

To order this book directly from the authors, contact Kent Julian at 770-339-8116 or kentjulian@earthlink.net

ISBN: 1-59052-064-5

www.newmosaicmedia.com
NEW MOSAIC MEDIA

Creating Missional Media For Your Ministry

What happens when the youth pastor and the church media guy spend way too much time together? You end up with new ministry resources that actually speak to this generation. New Mosaic Media exists to create missional media for cutting edge churches and youth ministries.

- Video Illustrations
- Motion Backgrounds
- Web Design
- Teaching Tools
- Logo Design
- Print Media (like the cover of this book)

Roy Baunsgard
church media guy

Matt Archer
youth pastor

for a free video illustration
go online now...

www.newmosaicmedia.com

NEW MOSAIC MEDIA

LEE TOWNS
Student Ministry Leader-Coach

STUDENT MINISTRY SPEAKING, PARENT SEMINARS
CONSULTING & TEAM DEVELOPMENT

FOR MORE INFORMATION:

leetowns@mac.com

501.351.5844

MIKE HARDER

Youth Ministry Event Speaker,
Youth Staff Training,
Ministry Consulting &
Team Development

Contact Information:
Mpharder1@aol.com
215-368-6263

Unknown by many, discovered by few, a communicator that is authentic in a culture that is ever changing and challenging...what?

Guy Wasko

"Truth is communicated and digested in different forms...my role is to join the process of presenting truth as a piece of the storytelling process, not the ONLY piece."

SPEAKER

CONSULTANT

TEACHER

STRATAGIST

TEAM BUILDER

FACILITATOR

BOWLER

FRIEND TO STRAYS

Guy is a relational, engaging communicator who uses his creativity and storytelling woven with truth to impact an audience, or at least keep them awake until food arrives. The point is...he doesn't take himself too seriously, which allows him to connect with people of all experiences and ages. As he says, "most people have the answers, they just need a hand discovering them." Guy is that missing ingredient for your next event.

CONTACT & ADDITIONAL INFO:
GUY@GUYWASKO.COM
WWW.GUYWASKO.COM

DESIGN & CREATIVE CONSULTATION - CHIP DAVID - WWW.KX3.COM

Kent Julian
author, youth speaker

Kent Julian is the national director for Alliance Youth, an organization that serves approximately 2,000 churches in the United States.

He speaks to youth workers and students across the country at retreats, conferences, and school assemblies and is available for your next event.

Adults and students alike appreciate Kent's authenticity, humor, story-telling, and passion.

Listen to what others are saying about Kent's presentations:

"Kent's as good as any 'big name' communicator out there, and very easy to work with. We asked Kent to do some very specific things at our conference and he delivered! We'll be asking him back again and again."
— **student ministries conference director**

"Kent's a great story-teller. The best speaker I've ever heard." — **middle school student**

"Kent had me laughing, crying, and caring all at the same time. He was the best speaker at this conference." — **high school student**

"Clear, relevant, passionate." — **youth pastor**

Interested in booking Kent Julian for your next event?
Contact him at: 770-339-8116 or email: kentjulian@earthlink.net